DISCOVERY IN WORD

DISCOVERY IN WORD

Readings Edited by **Robert Heyer, S.J.**

Viewpoints and Questions Written by **J. Brown**

Design by **Emil Antonucci**

Coordinated by **Richard J. Payne**

Editorial Assistance by **Daniel Gatti**

PAULIST PRESS
New York, N.Y. Paramus, N.J.

ASSOCIATION PRESS
New York, N.Y.

Published by Paulist Press
Editorial Office: 304 W. 58th St., N.Y., N.Y. 10019
Business Office: Paramus, New Jersey 07642
Association Press
291 Broadway
New York, N.Y. 10007

Printed and bound in the
United States of America

ACKNOWLEDGMENTS

Peanuts Cartoons
courtesy United Features Syndicate

New Yorker Cartoons
courtesy The New Yorker

Jules Feiffer Cartoons
courtesy of Publishers-Hall Syndicate

Crane Cartoons
courtesy of John Knox Press

Song "The Impossible Dream"
courtesy Sam Fox Music, Inc.

Catholic Bulletin
244 Dayton Avenue
St. Paul, Minnesota

P. Stevens
Headmaster
Williston Academy
East Hampton, Massachusetts

E. S. Wilson
Dean of Admissions
Amherst College
Amherst, Massachusetts

Rev. Janko Zayar, O.P.
Editor—Season
6172 Chabot Road
Oakland, California

Jane Witbread
524 East 84th Street
New York, New York

U.S. Catholic
221 West Madison Avenue
Chicago, Illinois

Mary S. Calderone
SIECUS
1790 Broadway
New York, New York

Redbook
230 Park Avenue
New York, New York

The Thomas More Association
180 North Wabash Avenue
Chicago, Illinois

Msgr. George W. Casey
United States Conference for
*   the World Council of Churches, Inc.*
475 Riverside Drive
New York, New York

Risk
Albert van den Heuvel

The New Yorker
25 West 43rd Street
New York, New York

Curtis Publishing Co.
Independence Square
Philadelphia, Pa.

Dr. Buell Gallagher
President
City College of New York

Rizzoli Press Service
via Civitavecchia 102
Milan, Italy

Association for International Development
374 Grand Street
Paterson, New Jersey

The New York Times

The Sign
Monastery Place
Union City, New Jersey

Ave Maria Press
Notre Dame, Indiana

Sacred Heart Messenger
211 East 87th Street
New York, New York

Listening
2570 Asbury Road
Dubuque, Iowa

Sheed and Ward, Inc.
64 University Place
New York, New York

C. D. B. Bryan

Sister M. J. O'Keefe

Rev. L. J. Evoy, S.J.

New Directions Publishing Corp.
33 Sixth Avenue
New York, New York

Harper & Row Publishers, Inc.
49 East 33rd Street
New York, New York

Time

Newsweek

World Institute Council

Direction
3109 South Grand Boulevard
St. Louis, Mo.

Time-Life Books

A.I.D. Dialogue
374 Grand Street
Paterson, New Jersey

ACT
Christian Family Movement
1655 West Jackson Boulevard
Chicago, Illinois

Cowles Education Corporation
488 Madison Avenue
New York, New York

United Press International

Look

J. B. Lippincott Company
East Washington Square
Philadelphia, Pa.

Jesuit Missions
211 East 87th Street
New York, New York

Catholic Mind
106 West 56th Street
New York, New York

America
106 West 56th Street
New York, New York

Center for Study of Democratic Institutions
Box 4427
Santa Barbara, California

National Catholic Reporter
P.O. Box 281
Kansas City, Mo.

CONTENTS

11

GENERAL INTRODUCTION

This book is for Christ and for the Catcher. It is written in the hope that all sorts of clowns and sometime-fakers will learn about this P. T. Barnum Circus of the Mind outside the church and synagogue doors before the time comes to decide how one must paint his face, and whether or not he will water the elephants—all for a taste of sawdust in the mouth and a worn parasol.

It is religious, I suppose, in the sense that it aspires to more than just the banal. We've copped out on Modern Youth and Chastity pamphlets. No answers in this book. Not even the eternal ones.

It is certainly no breviary, no prayer volume, although there are prayers in it. We simply forgot to include the Amens and the Hey Lords and the Thou Art Most Mercifuls, the red and blue ribbons to mark your place and the gold edges of each page. A small oversight—you will forgive us.

It's meant to be honest. We may, at times, have gotten sarcastic or angry, and at times our insights may not have been the most profound, but we have, to our knowledge, written nothing which is a lie.

The message of this book is a basic one. Life is either Mystery or absurdity. Find out about who you are, find out about pain and suffering, find out about peace and joy, find out about helping your brother who cries—like you and me: find out about loving, and you'll find out about the Mystery.

And that's the act of faith. Sorry, but it just had to be made. And in broad daylight, too. My, but what *is* this world coming to.

So read the articles, think about the questions and comments, and do your thing.

And I guess that's all. Except—

Be cool.

J Brown

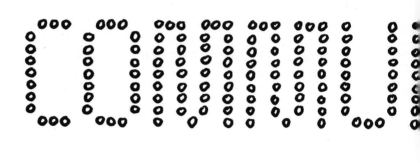

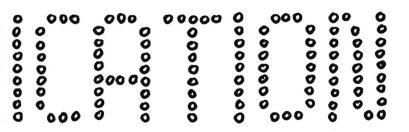

The sound of silence plays over radios, on record players, out of loudspeakers. It's called communication without meaning, words with empty syllables. The modern song laments it, the modern song exemplifies it. Smashing hard against the eardrums, it never enters, being impotent. And you see it, the sound of silence, on the stage, enacted, mourned. You hear it boom, like cymbals, truth crashing against illusion. You sit in a theater seat and Edward Albee will entertain you with *Who's Afraid of Virginia Woolf*. You listen. Martha says to George, "I've tried. I've really tried to reach you." George answers, "I'm sorry. I don't believe you." And you can hear it, inside you—the sound of silence.

Thoughts become determined by *The New York Times,* by the Playboy Advisor, by Christ. It's all the same. People mouthing prophesies and aphorisms, concepts and half-truths, not particularly understanding what it is they are saying, not particularly caring to understand. And no one else caring, too numb, anesthetized by the sound of their own silence, their own falsehoods told to themselves to live.

Paul Krassner once said of Lenny Bruce that he knew people used *The Prophet* to justify their own immorality. I suspect he did, and if he didn't, it doesn't really matter. Because it's still true—people do use *The Prophet* for that, and a lot of other things you wouldn't want to tell your mother about. Talk of the philosophy of love to a girl, and hope that when her senses are dulled enough and she really trusts you, you can use her. And when it's over, there's not much left but the sound.

And you can run to love, run to where there are two people who care very much for each other and are trying like hell to know if they're in love. Run to where there is need, to where there is hope, and you have not run away from it. The sound of silence doesn't fade easy, even where there is sincerity, even where there is desire.

Robert Frost wrote a poem, "The Hill Wife." There is a woman who has sat every day for years and watched her husband work in the fields, cut the wood, provide, who one day gets up and walks away, and never returns to him. One day, there was nothing, but the sound, and the echo.

Until honest and free communication is found between people, there can be no real brotherhood. And as two young people sit in the back seat of a 1965 Chevrolet, making out, for hours, because there is nothing to say, no other emotion to communicate, the sound of silence plays on the drive-in screen. Pass the popcorn, please.

Drawing by Saxon. © 1967 by *THE NEW YORKER MAGAZINE.* Used by permission.

YOUTH WITH ITSELF

Most students are children of the white collar and professional classes. But the new generation is throwing off the mores of their past. The middle class is preoccupied with status, security, personal restraint, moderation and success. The parents of the students "got ahead," and the students couldn't care less. They want something more alive and intense. They crave experience and they want to do something useful. For them, to live is to take risks and to be involved. To live is to act with meaning. And the action shocks the traditionalists, appalls parents —and sells newspapers.

Michael Otten, "The Meaning of Student Protest," *SEASON*, Fall, 1966. Reprinted in *CATHOLIC MIND*, April 1967, pp. 22–23.

"They [students] want something more alive and intense." What is this something? Does it fit in at all with the world of your parents?

"To live is to take risks and to be involved."

How do you take risks when you have a family to support and a job to keep and a down-payment on a car to meet? How do you find time to get involved when you have all the involvement you could want just making a living? These are some of the problems, and if you want to talk the truth, you have to face them. The reason, for the most part, parents aren't hip to the Love Generation is because they've been too busy producing it, nurturing it, and raising it. These things must be understood. But where understanding ought to be there is silence, charades, and dead argument.

What is the Love Generation, anyway?

Rob Carter is a twenty-year-old, shy, articulate, blond distillation of all that is most attractive in California youth. One evening in a private cove just south of Newport Beach, he and I watched the sunset while his parents were talking inside their beach house.

"The world is run by people over thirty," Rob said, "and we simply cannot trust them to morally rehabilitate themselves and their running the world. The big issues the young people deal with are mostly moral—a personal morality, a feeling for other people. That's where we're involved."

Rob Carter spoke so gently that it was often difficult to hear him over the surf. "We are unwarlike," he said. "We question why war is happening and what it does to people. I suppose most people over thirty have been indoctrinated to believe that war is right if our government says so. During the time the over-thirties formulated their ideas the concept of questioning authority wasn't there—they just accepted it."
The sun had set and now the wind coming at us from the ocean was cold.

"I think the main reason people my age think the way we do," Rob Carter was saying, "is because of the education received from people over thirty who taught us to question. We've learned from them a more rounded knowledge of history, sociology and so on, so that we've been made aware of a larger scope of humanity. And with mass communications we can see what is happening and what might happen. The education given us by older people is what taught us to question the ideals, the morality of the people leading us." Rob pulled up the collar of his thick Irish knit sweater. He said, "The difference between the over-thirties and us is that the older people weren't given the education we were. We were taught to think freely, and we do.

C. D. B. Bryan, "Why the Generation Gap Begins at 30," THE NEW YORK TIMES MAGAZINE July 2, 1967 pp. 34–35 © Copyright 1967 by the New York Times Company. Reprinted by permission.

> *Is what Rob Carter said what you want to say? Can you think of anything else that ought to be added? Or is there anything you don't really agree with, that you think isn't saying what you feel?*
>
> *Is that the difference—that you can think freely, while the older generation is caught up with rote obedience and conditioned nods? What is it to think freely?*

My only real regret about being over thirty is that when I was twenty I thought that the best way to behave was cool. How could I believe it was best—or even *possible*—to remain aloof from what is happening around me?

I wish ten years ago I had had the intelligence

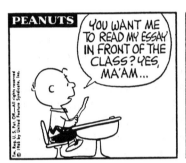

and courage that I see in so many of the twenty-year-olds today.

Most of the over-thirties I have spoken to have enormous respect for the young people who are involved who do place themselves in personal jeopardy. They are the nucleus of every worthy youthful movement. We are not so impressed by the average movement member. If a movement is happening and you are twenty you join it. At twenty one is always concerned with doing things which are popular among one's contemporaries. At thirty, contemporaries are not so important.

What are the major causes advocated by the new generation? Peace. Civil Rights. Love. Free Speech. What rational man isn't in favor of these causes? The point, however, is not that these causes are obvious but rather since they are obvious why is it the youth and not all of us who are involved? I'm afraid it's because a twenty-year-old, who has an awareness that an injustice or an immoral situation is being perpetrated, depends upon his involvement in the situation to understand it, as if through osmosis it were possible to gain enlightenment. The over-thirties have been in or seen enough situations, both just and injust, with or without credibility gaps, to know how difficult it is to ever know what is going on. At thirty, one has perspective—and cops out. But not always.

C. D. B. Bryan, "Why the Generation Gap Begins at 30."

What's cool?

He says, "At thirty, contemporaries are not so important." What does that mean?

"At thirty, one has perspective—and cops out." Is that the way it is, that when you see things a little better, a little clearer, you play for security and the easy life, and the anger becomes dulled by experience?

Is that why communication is so hard—it becomes a matter of idealism fighting against the insurmountable advantage of reality?

If you just went to high school for the curriculum, you would have just a book education. When you get involved you meet more people and it adds another dimension to your life. It's almost equally important, I think.

THE YOUNG AMERICANS p. 64. Reprinted by permission of Time-Life Books. Copyright 1966, Time Inc.

It is important to place a proper value on things.
To do this you must be able to understand yourself,
know what is important to you and what has meaning in your life.
What does it mean to communicate with yourself?
How much of a place do people *hold*
in your academic life?
Can you learn about yourself
by learning about others?

**Kids who run are desperate. Their view may be
lopsided, but as they see it, they are failures at school, at home,
or both, and there's nothing but failure ahead. Some runaways
are angry. Some say their parents don't understand or care.
Some are scared. They blame themselves. All are full of panic,
and the panic runs with them. It makes them vulnerable, eager
for any comfort or attention that's offered. Runaways often try
to punish their parents, but the hopeful ones . . . have values
and go off feeling that with time and distance they can learn
how to live by them.**
"Runaways" LOOK 7/25/67 p. 32.

Frustration can distort almost anything.
A teenager has not been taught how to deal with himself,
much less other people, and so in crisis the impulse is to run,
to get out. Can running away be a solution? Where do you run to?
If the teenager had been able to communicate
with his parents, with friends, had been able to loose inhibitions
and take off the masks, do you think running away would
still be the only answer? What is a prime cause of frustration?
What does it mean to "have values"?

YOUTH LOOKING AT YOUTH

**So many [teenagers] could really do something
for the world, but they're just sitting around doing nothing.
Magazines and newspapers seem to take two types of teenagers,
high-society types and hoodlums, and say "this is the American
teenager." They don't seem to think the middle and lower classes
have anything to offer. But this is the largest category, in between.**

22

the kids who don't have hot rods to run around in, but don't have to steal to eat. What I'm afraid of is that the teenagers of today, when they grow older, will be just like the adults of today. They don't let brotherly love come through. If that's the future, then the world's in pretty bad shape.
THE YOUNG AMERICANS p. 12.

"What I'm afraid of is that the teenagers of today, when they grow older, will be just like the adults of today." What is the one thing that will assure his fear being realized?

How good is the communication among teenagers themselves? Do they understand each other, or is that a game too, mouthing lines from both Dylans and paying empty verbal homage to Kahlil Gibran and Jesus Christ, and filling in the lull in the conversation with, "Isn't The Lord of the Rings *tremendous?"*

When you talk deep (as it is so called) are you really trying to transfer an idea, an emotion, to another person, or are you just doing a good imitation of what you think someone deep should say?

What does he mean when he says, "They don't let brotherly love come through"?

I never have gotten along with other kids. Why should I want to be just a nice American teenager and go around with nice American teenage friends? I'm branded with being a cynic and a snob. But I really get the feeling that life can be a grubby place. You have to do something about it to make yourself happy.
THE YOUNG AMERICANS p. 16.

You must have felt that way sometime—tired of your friends and tired of yourself because you're so much like them. And you want to get out of the clique but it's fun to be in, and you've come to depend on it in a way. Like you have to live with other people, and you can't just cross them off. Yeah.

Is it a detriment to communication to think "other kids" are just "nice American teenagers"? Are other kids just nice American teenagers? If so, what makes you think you're not just a "nice American teenager" for the other guy, and be sure he doesn't want to have you for a friend?

Isn't it possible that the greatest threat to communication among teenagers is making a judgment on others before you've gotten to know them?

What is the danger of tags like "teenybopper" and "collegiate"?

Beatlemania has strengthened our faith, our beliefs and our hopes in not only ourselves but in you and him and her and them and everyone. We're not asking for much because we already have a lot. Naturally we defend our beatlemania as legitimate and good. We've already found out that life is good. Our next step is to live it.
THE YOUNG AMERICANS p. 71.

Is this attitude naive?

Do phenomenons such as beatlemania and flower power help teenagers understand each other better?

"We've already found out that life is good."
Is this a general feeling among most teenagers?

YOUTH LOOKING AT PARENTS AND ADULTS

Charlie B., 17, is one of the most popular boys in the senior class. A smile rarely leaves his face. It leaves when he talks about his father.

"My father has his own problems, and I don't expect him to devote all his spare time to me or to understand all of what I want to do. But I ought to get a few credits from him. I volunteered last summer to tutor some poor kids in reading in a town near here. My father laughed when I told him, and said if I were smart, I'd earn some money. We don't need the money, and he didn't want any of what I would have earned. But I wasn't getting paid for tutoring, so it was no good.

"Two years ago, a group of us went to a school basketball game. It was a rough game with a lot of heckling. On the way home, two guys from the other school jumped my

best friend. They really began pounding him. The other two
in my group just watched. I couldn't stand there and let my friend
watch me watch him getting hurt. So I jumped in to help him.
I was cut up pretty badly. When I got home, my parents were sore.
They couldn't understand why I had to interfere. About six years
ago, I ran away. We were driving home from my grandfather's
funeral—my mother's father—and my father criticized my
grandfather. On the way home from the man's funeral.
I didn't say anything, but I left that night and stayed away
three days."

YOUTH QUAKE p. 50 © 1967 Cowles Communications, Inc., in
cooperation with United Press International and the Editors of LOOK.

Between parents and teenagers there is a split
in values. Youth argues virtue, adults argue practicality.
Youth quotes Christ, Buddha, and what their ideals dictate.
Adults quote newspapers, magazines, and what their eyes have seen.
How can the teenager talk to his parents
when both points of view are so totally different? Is there any
common area on which they can meet?

Ideally it would be great to have a closer
relationship with my parents, but I don't talk to them much.
Recently we have been arguing about haircuts and homework.
I've had a lot of fights with my mother; she'll always be nagging.
And my dad will get mad when I don't expect him to.
I've had only a few heart-to-heart talks with my dad in my
whole life. Adults are not in touch with us and what we do.
They are always assuming they are right. They usually classify
teenagers as a group, and I do not like being stamped as one
of a large group when nobody bothers to find out whether I am
a person. It's the adults' world right now. They control it—
schools, even our clothes, our home and all communications;
we have very little to say about how the world is run.
We're just sort of outsiders right now.

THE YOUNG AMERICANS p. 42.

"I don't talk to them much." The idea is to talk
with your parents, to make your point as clearly as you can

W Miller

and then listen to theirs. Don't get bitchy and play put-ons.
That achieves nothing. If they just don't understand, and you're
tired of hearing "Well, you have to admit, son, that your mother
and I *have* lived a lot longer than you have," then try to play it
so you can get on without hurting them, until the time comes
when things have mellowed, or you are old enough to make it
on your own. But the truth is what is, and they have, as a matter
of fact, lived a lot longer than you have. This doesn't mean
they understand you, but it probably does mean that they
understand the world you've got to live in, and which the
average American youth has only a vague notion of. You can
know things are lousy and corrupt, but that's not to say you know
how to go about paying bills on a new house and raising a
family that needs a lot of love and looking after. In some cases
at least, and only the person can judge them, lack of experience
should yield the benefit of the doubt.

"I do not like being stamped as one of a large group
when nobody bothers to find out whether I am a person."

Are you? A person I mean. Because the last time
I asked you, out came the defense and up went the hands.
"Hey, look—just don't try to pin me down." And you went over
to sulk in the corner and play chords on your guitar (or flip
baseball cards with yourself or whatever you do over in a corner
sulking).

"You don't know how it is, man."
"Okay, then how is it?"
"I don't know. I mean I can't explain it. You know."
"Yeah. I know."
And here's the way it is:
Now y'see, before I met this girl when I was
fifteen, the only person I ever really talked to was a kid in school.
We were sitting down on the steps and he asked me if he could
ask me something, and I said Sure. He wanted to know if girls
masturbate. I didn't know, but we started talking, and I told him
all sorts of things about what I felt. We talked for a long time.
And when I saw him the next day, it was no good. Like we
knew too much about each other. We didn't talk like that
anymore. It was no good.

Nobody really cares, you find that out. Your time
comes for your 15 minutes in the Student Counselor's office,
and he talks about what you ought to do in life, like you're not
even there and he's talking to the whole student body heart to heart.

And he doesn't know you want to talk about being lonely,
or how sometimes you can't cry and you want to, really bad.
But he wouldn't understand.
          And how many times were you with somebody
who really gave a damn about what you had to say,
about your girl and about the game? Twice?
          Look. Nobody cares. You find that out.
You find that out pretty damn quick in this world.
          O.K. But if you want people to care, you have to
start by caring about *them*. Listen to them, find what's good
in them, understand their faults. If you brood, if you turn cynical,
if you really couldn't give a damn about anybody else,
you're a drag. And nobody will care very much whether or not
you want to be stamped as part of one large group.
It's just taken for granted.

          I think that parents have some mistaken ideas
about what we're like. Whenever they want to find out about kids,
they go off to some specialist. We like to read these observations
of sociologists. They assume that if one particular bunch of
teenagers acts this way, they all do. We laugh. If they'd just go
to the teenagers. We'd tell them. I'm not average. I'm not typical.
But I'm not typically unusual either. . . . I'm immature,
plenty. But I have faith in man. It irritates me that people
don't have more confidence in other people.
THE YOUNG AMERICANS p. 7.

          What are some of the mistaken ideas that parents
have about teenagers? And then how are you going to set them
straight, let them know you had the same dreams they had,
and you don't want your *ideals and* your *dreams to go the same*
route theirs did, bunched up and smothered in a 9 to 5
"Penny Lane" blanket. By faking it, by playing into a role
some sociologist synthesized out of graphs and predetermined
observations? By living up to those mistaken ideas, and giving them
credence? Okay, then again the question—how?
How are you going to communicate?

"It irritates me that people don't have confidence in other people." Well what do you expect, with child rapers and every kind of jerk walking the street. I wouldn't trust a nun. I wouldn't trust my Uncle George. They're all thieves, they're all out to make a buck. There's nobody in this lousy world who wouldn't use you if they thought that they could get away with it. Your Christ didn't know that. Confidence? You have confidence in your apple-pie-and-gray-suit fellow man and he'll turn around and kick you in the teeth. And talk to him? What the hell does he want to know about you? The only thing he wants to know is how much of a sucker he can play you for. Am I right? You tell me, am I right or ain't I?
A High School Senior.

I want to stop being a child as soon as I can, I've always preferred to talk to adults—you can trust them more, I think. My relationship with my parents was very much an eye-level sort of thing.
THE YOUNG AMERICANS p. 16.

". . . you can trust them [adults] more, I think." You can also buy a button for 25¢ that says don't trust anyone over thirty. Which one do you agree with? The first is a result of parents treating this girl with respect, this "eye-level sort of thing," and the second could be a result of adults treating children as inferior creatures. The feeling engendered in the home is the feeling carried away by the child. If there is love, the child will grow up capable of loving; if there is anger, there will be an angry child. So if there is trust between the parents and the child, the child will grow up knowing how to trust others, and only through trust can there be communication. Without trust there are only games.

[The teen subculture] is a language and moves against adults, or at best excluding them, as if they were a foreign tribe, probably hostile. In principle, every teenager is a delinquent. Little communication can occur between the generations. Embarrassment becomes withdrawal if not sullenness, and indifference results from diffidence. A major part of the

subculture, in schools, is to nullify the whole processing system by distraction, cheating and conspiring to be stupid.
THE YOUNG AMERICANS pp. 18–19.

"In principle, every teenager is a delinquent."
What does this mean? Is it a put-down, or merely an observation?
Is it true?

"Little communication can occur between the
generations." What about you? Can you honestly say you discuss
things other than Red China and football with your father,
and where you're going this Friday night while your mother
serves you dinner? Can you do this without making an effort,
and feeling like you want to go to your room and do something
else, like go to sleep? Is indifference the answer, just turning
yourself off and mumbling a few words when the conversational
ball is thrown to you? Or is it possible that if you make the effort,
after a while it becomes enjoyable to talk to your mother and
your father? What about it? What do you think? Does it work?

"Embarrassment becomes withdrawal if not
sullenness. . . ." There are some things that if you told your
parents you did them or thought them, it would hurt your mother,
and anger your father. So you are ashamed, and remain silent,
in time about everything. And all the things your parents think
you are, all their blue-eyed visions of a good, honest son or
daughter make you feel guilty. And guilt has a three-day-old
beard of lies. You cannot communicate, you cannot hope to
communicate if you are trying to hide something with lies.
And the saddest part of all is, ten to one, there is nothing to be
guilty about, even if you think you are a sex-maniac or some
kind of pervert.
A High School Senior.

But ask the bewildered adult, why all the noise
and horrible twanging guitars? A quote from Bob Dylan,
"The only beauty's ugly, man," would give a clue. . . .
There is also a feeling young people have of living in a world
of loudness, a culture of noise from the freeways and jets,

I think I'm lost here.

**where quiet and privacy can be found only in the midst of sound,
as in the eye of a hurricane.**
THE YOUNG AMERICANS p. 70.

"There is also a feeling . . . of living in
a world of loudness." Sometimes a person has to be by himself,
and he doesn't want to communicate with anybody, just for a while.
It's a time to get his thoughts in order, or maybe take a rest
from thinking and blow his mind. And since pastures and fields
of daffodils that dance are at a premium these days, the peace
that blasting music brings (in that it cuts off the other sounds
of reality like cars and crying babies and basketball coaches
yelling "Run!") is an oasis. And it must be understood that they
may have a difficult time understanding, but who ever said
communication is easy. Take the time to explain to them what
the loudness is for, and if it doesn't do any good, at least you tried.

". . . privacy can be found only in the midst of sound . . ."

Marshall McLuhan is of the opinion that all privacy has
been broken down in our society. Where can you find
privacy? When you see your most intimate functions and
secrets in black and green lettering on a smudged subway platform
poster, do you really feel like saying much about yourself
to anyone? Why should you? It's up there for them to read.
And the result is you're probably trying to hold on to any remnant
of your human mystique (if you seriously believe it exists)
that's been left, after the most indelicate rape by hidden persuasion.
You become silent, aloof. There is no communication, no desire
to communicate. And then what is left?

**We are terrified because some youngsters
seem to understand that the world they live in is a part of
their business and are trying to attend to it by taking aggressive
positions on social issues ranging from school policy to foreign
policy; and we ask, "Why are young people getting so rebellious?"**
THE YOUNG AMERICANS p. 86.

*Is this the reason parents are worried, even terrified
—that youth are involved? Or is it that this involvement is
accompanied by violence, apathy, cynicism, long hair and beards?*

Is the inconsistency of youth the real problem that must be communicated, the continual changing, the bad with the good, the immaturity in some things and the clearly mature attitude in others? Does a teenager understand this himself? And isn't it really a reciprocal thing, between parent and teenager, each learning and communicating? What are your thoughts?
Is communicating with your parents important to you?

"Some kids think their parents ignore their needs and like them only for the status value of their achievements. They are eager to believe that free and spontaneous feeling is pure love."
"Runaways" LOOK 7/25/67 p. 29.

Are you measured by the number of trophies you win, the degree of praise you are accorded at the Parent-Teachers' Meeting, the attractiveness of your girl friend?
Do your parents have the same idea of love that you have? Are the ways they express love the ways you want to express love? Have you ever asked your parents about what love means to them?

YOUTH LOOKING AT CHURCH AND PARISH

What zealous young people of the "new left" really want is to establish a community of love and knowledge where citizens share concern with passionate responsibility. This, actually, is what the Church is—a community of love and knowledge, at once more human and more universal than any city founded by men. But the disaffected young do not recognize it as such a community. They are frightened by its structure— as if it were a monolithic corporation run by old men. . . . They feel they grow closer to the experience of community in "the movement" than they do at worship.
AMERICA, Editorial, Sept. 17, 1966 p. 271.

How would you define "passionate responsibility"?
Do you find the Church "a community of love

and knowledge"? Or is it instead a parade of novenas and miraculous medals? If you were to establish a community of people bonded together by a common belief in something, and a willingness to die for that belief, what would you hold as the most important factors to keep your community intact?

Is love within the Church being successfully communicated?

Why are the young "disaffected"? That is to say, why, if at all, do you feel disaffected?

Would you rather be helping a kid younger than yourself learn to read than attending Sunday Mass, or going to Sunday prayer meetings? Which one means more? Why?

For us Catholics the parish is the spiritual post office, the spiritual supermarket, the spiritual movie house or bowling parlor; and we have the same community as the customers at the post office or the A&P. We may even have the community of the passengers on the Evanston Express—all going to the same place by the same means without knowing each other or being concerned with each other.
John L. McKenzie, S.J. "Q.E.D." THE CRITIC, April–May 1967, pp. 10–11.

You can find about as many John-loves-Mary's enclosed in crooked hearts carved into the Church pew as you can find carved into the Quaker benches in the local coffee house. And it is, at best, dubious that the graffiti on the Church pew is a New Testament reference. This defacement is not really a sign of irreverence, although it has been taken as such for some time. It is rather a testimonial to the attitude which many Christians have for their community, and its religious symbol, the Church. Are the services performed by the Church simply another commodity? What does this have to do with communication?

Do you feel toward church and religion with essentially the same impersonal outlook as you do toward the post office and the U.S. government?

Do you feel any closer bond with the people around you at Sunday services than you feel with the people

I'll meet you halfway
—from the middle.

around you at the movie house? Does the action of the movie screen create a more mutual emotion than worship creates among the faithful in church?

Our parishes are closed societies, and that is why they are not Christian communities. The Christian community is an open society by definition; its outlook is as broad as the outlook of Jesus Christ, who died to save all men. We have much in common with the Pharisees, to whom also we are often unfair; at least it seems unfair to traduce those from whom one has borrowed so much.

How are we to open this society? This is not a matter of organization and structure; it is a matter of persons. What has to be opened is minds. It means more than the fact that the Church is open to anyone; we all know this, but openness means more than a readiness to accept converts. It means a readiness to accept those who are not converts. We accept them as persons, as those who Jesus has said are identified with him, as those in whom we find God. Our concern touches the entire community, not just its Catholic members.

John L. McKenzie, S.J. "Q.E.D," THE CRITIC April–May 1967, p. 12.

What is meant by a closed society? Do you think your parish is closed off, shut in? What means can be taken concretely to open up the parishes, make them once again Christian communities?

Is lack of communication between parishes and those outside parishes a possible cause of ill feeling and misunderstanding between Christians and those of other faiths?

"What has to be opened is minds." Preconceived ideas, prejudices, and feelings of superiority have been a dead weight on the backs of progressive Christians for decades. You can call someone a Christ-killer till you're blue in the face, but it achieves nothing. And just because some Protestants don't particularly feel affection for the Blessed Virgin, it doesn't mean that they're ignorant and antichrists. And because Catholics claim infallibility for their Pope doesn't mean they are absolutely close-minded. Even the atheist, who

has been labeled everything from a friend of Satan to a lousy
pinko, even he, believe it or not, has a lot to say
that is true, and many times much more eloquently than your
Father O'Reilly at the ten o'clock Mass. If a person does
not open his mind, he cannot ever hope to open his heart.
Love for the Christian is not hermitage: it is giving, inwardly and
outwardly.

> *If our basic problem is communication,
> how can we find ways of listening to one another in order to
> understand each other's way of looking at the Church?*
> *Is it enough to just listen to other views? Certainly
> it's a beginning, and a long overdue commencement at that,
> but what must come after dialogue, if dialogue is to have any
> value at all?*

**The parish in which I live is not dying. I fear it
has died. The needs of my neighbors are amazing. One is a
sense of security in their local parish leaders. But after having
been brought into the Church, they fill out the "forms," as
one admitted to a hospital would.**
A High School Junior.

> *"The needs of my neighbors are amazing."*
> *What are some of these needs?*

**I think the real symbols of Christian reality
in my parish or any other are the people. But on the other hand,
I wonder. Is Christian reality becoming the size of the church,
contributions for the Cardinal's campaign, etc. . . ? These
things are becoming more and more evident. The person who
donates the most money is first in Christian reality.**
A High School Junior.

**You want to believe the Church is people, but
too often what comes across is not that at all. Green-felt-on-
straw collection baskets and Sunday envelopes that look like**

"My mother probably thinks we're out necking or something."

lottery tickets: it tends to confuse.
A High School Senior.

> *What do you think is first in Christian reality? Is there such a thing as "first" in Christianity at all?*

I want a Church I can believe in, one that can recognize its own mistakes as well as those of its members . . . I don't want a Church that says we should enter into dialogues with God because you can't define either dialogue or God in that context. This may be the "intellectual" era, pseudo or real, but if we try to view God on a truly intellectual level, we'll either lose our minds or, as is obvious, fail. I want a Church which looks at God for what He is, namely, God, our maker, the end all and be all of what we are and whatever we will be.
A High School Senior.

It is not so easy to get caught up in an argument over religion and the subtleties that separate God from the Prima Causa. When theologians start using "this-seems-to-be-so" and "it-is-difficult-to-really-define" verbal cop-outs, the layman himself begins to wonder if it all isn't just speculation, and that his guess is as good as anybody's, including Thomas Aquinas'.
A High School Senior.

> *"I want a Church which looks at God for what he is, namely, God . . ." Do you think the writer has any definite idea of what God really is for him? Do you think he is shutting himself off? Why is this a detriment to communication?*

I guess what I really want from the Church is some answers about my existence. I want the Church to answer my questions with answers that I can accept. I want or need answers to such questions as: "What purpose is there to my life?" or "Is my life as futile as it seems to be at times?" I want a Church that is able to console you when you need consolation, a warm and human Church . . . A Church should be under-

standing and loving, aware of human weaknesses, a forgiving
thing instead of a wrathful, righteous thing . . . When I say
these things about my Church I guess I'm saying what I want my
God to be, since they all are the same.
A High School Senior.

Is he right—are the Church and God the same?
Why is communication so important to someone
like this?

PARENTS, ADULTS UNDERSTANDING YOUTH

Some adults feel threatened by the negative
response of young people to authority because they interpret
it as contempt or outright disregard for the law. Yet, what is really
involved is the adult-adolescent relationship, not law versus
lawlessness. Pre-teens and adolescents are more prone to ask
"Why?" than they used to be. Perhaps we should be grateful for
their questioning. We adults ourselves asked "Why?" when we
were their age—but we didn't always have the courage to put
the question openly.
George H. Moreau, O.M.I. "Why Teenagers Have Problems,"
THE SIGN, March, 1967, p. 11.

The classic television bit of the fifties was an
advertisement for an encyclopedia, in which the young kid asks
his father, "Daddy, why is the sky blue?" Of course the old
man doesn't have any idea why the sky is blue and has to hit
the encyclopedia for the answer, thus hinting to all the good fathers
across America that if they don't want to look stupid in front
of their chidren, they'd better pick up this encyclopedia
quick. In the sixties, the questions are a little tougher though,
and when a young child asks, "Daddy, why is there hate?"
there is no pat little paragraph in a bound volume to answer him.
So you find a generation programmed (if you
will excuse the word) to expect the neat phrase and the Ben
Franklinism, becoming hostile and disillusioned because the whole
thing has been a lie. And so at the heels of Holden Caulfield,
they too are lost, still asking "Why?" and mistrusting anything
the people who live with clichés and aphorisms tell them.

How long do you think you'll ask "Why?" before it doesn't matter anymore?

We don't have the same closeness that existed between parents and children years ago. I think parents today should look back and ask themselves honestly how they look to their children. There are many, many homes today where the parent-child relationship is distant or strained or uncommunicative. Years ago the family had dinner together every evening. Many families today seldom eat together. The teenagers in many families do not ask their friends to stay over-night as house guests or to join the family for dinner. Instead the youngsters get a phone call or hear a horn honking outside—and off they go, away from the home! There is nothing for them in the home. The home is no longer a haven for teenagers.

George H. Moreau, O.M.I. "Why Teenagers Have Problems,"
THE SIGN, March, 1967, p. 12.

How much time do you spend at night home with
your family? Do you enjoy the time you spend at home, or
are you there because you have to be or because you have nothing
better to do?
Do you think that the breakdown of the family
unit has been a major cause of the lack of communication between
parents and children?

You are supposed to be free.
To love whoever, to be whoever.
But sometimes it doesn't work that way.
Sometimes it's not even close.
Too bad.
Because really, you *are* supposed to be free,
and when you're not free, you're not very happy.
The dentist told me I should brush my teeth.
But I'm free. I don't *gotta* brush my teeth.
Then you'll get cavities, and toothaches, and
false teeth. And when you get a toothache, you're not free to do
what you want. Because it hurts like hell. And when you have
false teeth, you're not free to eat what you want. They fall out.
Now if you had brushed your teeth . . .
But that means I'm only free when I've done
the things I'm supposed to do.
Yup.
Well what kind of freedom is that?
The only kind.
The facts are, freedom and responsibility are
inseparable. If you want to be free to find yourself, the truth, etc.,
then you have to accept responsibility. Like brushing your teeth.
Like caring about other people. Like giving.
You are supposed to be free.
To love whoever, to be whoever.
Some people aren't very free at all.
They choose not to be.
They cop out. On responsibility. On themselves.
Too bad.
Really.
Too bad.

44

FREEDOM AND SELF

Young men . . . extremely alienated, almost unbelievably so were it not that many of us know a few just like them. They are against everything, including themselves. Believing that commitment to an ideal, to one's life work, to a family or to a cause inevitably destroys freedom, the alienated are committed to nothing. They are true "rebels without a cause" and searchers without goals. They reject adulthood, for they feel it demands destructive commitments and results in loss of freedom and spontaneity.
"The Uncommitted," in a book review by W. Kenkel, AMERICA, January 22, 1966.

Freedom . . . is inwardness, spontaneity, the capacity of a man to find within himself the reasons and the motives of his own right decisions and action, apart from external coercion. Freedom therefore is authenticity, truthfulness, fidelity to the pursuit of truth and to the truth when found. In further consequence, freedom is experienced as duty, as responsibility —as a response to the claims of justice, to the demands of rightful law, to the governance and guidance of legitimate authority. In its intimately Christian sense, however, freedom has a higher meaning than all of this. Freedom, in the deepest experience of it, is love. To be free is to be-for-the-others. The Christian call to freedom is inherently a call to community, a summons out of isolation, an invitation to be-with-others, an impulse to service of the others.
John Courtney Murray, S.J. "Freedom, Authority and Community" AMERICA, Dec. 3, 1966.

Does responsibility, to yourself and to others, result in loss of freedom and spontaneity?

No man is as different from another man as he is different from himself at another time.
Pascal.

"It's my jacket. My mother <u>made</u> me wear it."

You are the protagonist. The plot is your life. The conflict is internal. The student in the back of the room is waving his hand for recognition. The teacher calls on him. "The protagonist is not consistent," he shouts, "his actions are sporadic." And therefore, the assumption is, you are not true to life, and a poor protagonist.

But you are not a novel; your life is not a poem. And if you expect it to be, you're going to be frustrated and eventually they're going to find you crawling the wall in a downtown bistro. Self-identity is coming to terms with yourself, learning who you are in relation to everything else. Sometimes you do things you didn't want to do and had no intention of doing. You tell lies that weren't worth telling, and that give you a used feeling for having told them. But that is part of it. You have to channel the emotions, and ultimately free yourself from the petty and illogical personal hang-ups, to concentrate on the ones that matter.

What does finding one's own identity have to do with freedom?

How do other people fit into your own search for self-identity?

How does God fit in? Or does He fit in at all?

What does love have to do with finding one's own identity?

Can one find it without love? Can one find it without other people?

Without God?

Sometimes you're just scared to be different if a lot of kids are going to mock you out.
THE YOUNG AMERICANS p. 50.

The decision is not whether to conform or not to conform. It's rather the crisis of personal freedom, to be free enough to understand that conformity is a misnomer and has no meaning in your life. The free man is one who is not concerned as to whether he conforms or not to ideals and patterns set up by others. He has the discipline of conscience, not of rules.

He who places others in formulated phrases, he who seeks
to label, he who makes it his business to constrict thoughts
and feelings of sensitive human beings—the free man—does
not let them push him into a mold. Their judgments and mock-outs
are something apart from the personalized experiences he tried
to place himself in.

*Some say that conformity is an aid to finding
self-identity, in that a person can see himself in others. Is this valid?*

*Besides conforming and not conforming, there
is a third choice. What is it?*

*If you believe life is a game, then why play by
somebody else's rules? Play by your own, and if you see the old
royal shaft coming, fall back into line until things have
cooled off.*

What does this have to do with self-identity?

*What are some of the ways in which people acquire
knowledge of themselves?*

*Isn't concern with conforming or not conforming
a lack of faith in yourself? Discuss.*

**In a world as messy as ours in 1967, the rebels'
idealism soon sours into cynicism, then frustration, then
negativism. It is one thing to condemn the world one's fathers
have made, and something else to seek a superior alternative,
especially when the world provides so many easily available
and superficially exciting diversions. It is one thing to tell a
College President that the rules are too restrictive and another to
tell him which rules should be improved so that the school
can improve its work and provide students a better education.
Thus, the rebel student, finding no engrossing
challenge in attending classes, rejecting the value system of his
elders, and not committed to a viable system of his own devising,
is at the mercy of the random selection of historical events. At
the moment, he identifies with the pockets of poverty, with
the racially oppressed, with the victims of Vietnam. But by and
large college rebels' ideals have proven transitory, lacking
the strength of the Utopian conviction that the rebels can and
will make things better.**

Buell Gallagher, "Our Students Have No Utopia," THE
SATURDAY EVENING POST.

What ideals have turned into cynicism in your life?
Do the ideals you have measure up to what
you want to be, and be known as? Do you believe you can
keep your ideals and make money at the same time?
What are some things which you disagree with in the
money system of adults?
How do you intend to obtain security without the
loss of your code of values?

FREEDOM AND HIPPIES

Difficult as it is to take precise bearings on the
hippies a salient feature stands out. They are predominantly
white, middle-class, educated youths, ranging in age from
17 to 25 (though some as old as 50 can be spotted). Overshadowed
with all the qualities that make their generation so engaging,
perplexing and infuriating, they are drop-outs from a way of
life that to them seems wholly orientated toward work, power
and status. They scorn money—they call it "bread"—and
other property and have found like countless other romantics
from Rimbaud to George Orwell, that it is not easy to starve.
Above all as Senator Robert Kennedy ("the best of a bad lot" to
hippies) puts it: "They want to be recognized as individuals,
but individuals play a smaller and smaller role in society. This
is a formidable and forbidding arrangement."

To alter that arrangement, the hippies hope to
generate an entirely new society, one rich in spiritual grace
that will revive the old virtues of agape and reverence. They
reveal, says University of Chicago theologian Dr. Martin E. Marty,
"the exhaustion of a tradition: Western, production-directed,
problem-solving, goal-orientated and compulsive in its way of
thinking." Marty refuses to put the hippies down as just another
wave of "creative misfits"; he sees them rather as spiritually
motivated crusaders striking at the values of straight society
where it is most vulnerable: its lack of soul. In a sense hippiedom
is a transplanted *Lost Horizon,* a Shangri-La à go-go blending
Asian resignation with American optimism in a world where
no one grows old.

It is in the hope of settling that precious state,
and defining his position in it, that the hippie uses drugs—
first for kicks, then as a kind of sacrament. Anti-intellectual,

49

distrustful of logic, and resentful of the American educational process, the hippie drops out—tentatively at first—in search of another more satisfying world.

"The standard thing is to feel in the gut that middle-class values are all wrong," says a West Coast hippie. "Like the way America recognizes that Communism is all wrong." They feel "up tight" (tense and frightened) about many desperate things—from sex to the draft, college grades to thermonuclear war. Hallucinogenic drugs like marijuana and LSD, they believe, are the knives that cut those knots. Once unleashed, most hippies become insatiable hedonists, smoking, and eating whatever can turn them on in a hurry; making love, however with whomever they can find (including "group grope" that "feels good and don't hurt nobody"): saturating the sense with music and color, light and motion until, like an overloaded circuit, the mind blows into the never-never land of selflessness. The middle-class ego, to the hippie, is the jacket that makes society straight, and must be destroyed before freedom can be achieved. One East Coast hippie recently held a "funeral" for his former self. "You must follow the river inside you to its source," he said, "and then out again."
TIME July 7, 1967 p. 19.

Is the hippie copping out, or is he trying to establish a new society, where the freedom of the individual is respected, and community is a way of life?

If he is copping out, who is he copping out on? If his act is a positive one, what kind of future does it have?

How would you define selflessness?

Why are things common both to the hippie life and the Christian life, or at least these ways of life in theory?

Do you think some hippies have more faith in their fellow man than a lot of Christians?

Where, if anywhere, do you think the hippies go wrong?

FREEDOM AND EDUCATION

I have given freedom a place of its own for I believe the secondary schools can do more to condition students to freedom than is now being done. Also the problem is a little easier to define than the emotional one.

To point up the problem of freedom consider the public school senior, male or female, who for the past eighteen years has been more or less controlled and directed by family, school and community presses. If a student began to slip in academic achievement, school and home often moved in together with extra study halls, detention, tutors, and limitations on freedom—such as no radio, T.V., or use of the family car. The allowance might even be cut or dollar rewards promised for improvement! These penalties or bribes would be continued until the student brought his work back to expectations.

The student is often forbidden in school and home to smoke or drink. Dates must be held in the family living room while Dad is in the next room watching television. All dates must terminate at a "decent" hour. On school days the student picks up his room each day, does some chores, wears proper shoes and clothes, gets a haircut on time, and grows no beard. With "Big Daddies" watching, the road of behavior is straight and narrow.

The independent boarding school student in his girlless world has many of the same limitations placed on his freedom plus ten roll calls or checks a day to make certain he is still on the school grounds. Naturally, nothing so upsets the headmaster as the news that one of his boys has escaped to freedom.

Three months after school graduation, this same wing-tied student is dropped onto the college campus with the wing ties removed. With little or no preparation for this freedom, he begins to flap his wings. Now in most institutions he can smoke and drink as much as he wants. Drinking is, of course, unlawful for citizens under twenty-one, but some friendly upperclassman or "townee" is always ready to help him out for a small pittance or a swig.

Our fledgling college student can now wear any kind of clothes (or lack of them if he is a she.) He can go barefoot, wear homemade sandals, grow a beard if he can, let his hair flow over his shoulders and dye it varying colors if he wishes. No one will criticize him except that "square" down the hall. This is no problem for no one likes him anyway.

He doesn't have to rise for breakfast or go to any other meals unless he wants to. He may go to the movies any

You certainly didn't expect adjusting to be easy, did you?

night; date every night. Class attendance may not be required, and if it is, cuts are always allowed. Assignments are mostly long-range so there is no pressing need to do any studying at once, and he can have girls in his room with the door shut. Not for all night, of course, but for many hours or at least long enough to read aloud a few short stories or play a few records!

When you consider the abruptness of the change from the controlled secondary school community to the rather uncontrolled life in a college community it is amazing that there are so few drop-outs.

You might expect me to suggest as a remedy that juniors and seniors in secondary school be given the same freedom that they will get in college. I am tempted to do so and my temptation was re-enforced by an item last month in *The New York Times* which reported that the head of the oldest nudist colony in Argentina bemoaned a lack of interest in nudism by the young. Said he, "Every one of us is now over forty-five years old and apparently the young people have many other interests which distract them these days."

Certainly if the secondary school students were permitted to dress as they wished, to grow beards or manly manes, they might in college rebel against all these imaginative expressions of individuality and become models of appearance and behavior. I said they might. These stories we hear about experimentation in the secondary school and even in junior high schools—experimentation involving liquor, dope, and sex— lead me to suspect that perhaps in one generation our college students will have drunk so deeply from the cup of life that they will find relief by throwing themselves into their academic life. Could this be possible?

Seriously, you secondary school leaders must continue to search for new ways to give students responsibility to make decisions in freedom. Dare to let them make a few bad choices and experience the unhappy consequences. Urge parents to unite with you in an attempt to lessen the wide gap that now exists for many students between the control of school and family (permissive homes exempted) and the freedom of college.

Some independent schools have begun to give students (particularly seniors) additional freedom—freedom to go to town, to stay up late, to try independent study with long-range assignments, to cut an occasional class for project work, etc. More must be done, and hopefully some suggestions will come from this conference.

With the freedom must come a chance for students to learn that freedom survives only when individual and group responsibility flourish. . . .

Are we who are educating young men and women to live in a self-governing society not missing an opportunity to introduce them to the hard choices of freedom and the responsibilities of self-government?

E. S. Wilson "Freedom Kills Whom? or How To Prepare Students To Drop Out." 1966 National Education Conference.

"With 'Big Daddies' watching, the road of behavior is straight and narrow." To what extent are you conditioned to depend on your parents for control and discipline in your life?

". . . continue to search for new ways to give students responsibility to make decisions in freedom." What ways can you suggest?

". . . freedom survives only when individual and group responsibility flourish." Explain.

What are some of the responsibilities of self-government?

If a student is generally cooperative and if he exhibits positive behavior, then his haircut is not a school problem. But if the haircut is part of his rebellious and aggressive tendencies, we try to counsel with the youngster.
ACT June, 1967.

This attitude toward discipline in schools represents a maturing process in school administration, getting away from the code book demerits and the browbeating conformity, which was apparently felt necessary for the curriculum to be effective. To place confidence in a youth is, more often than not, to cultivate confidence and, ultimately, a sense of integrity. The freedom of the individual is respected, and that respect gains respect.

**Schools should be less concerned with un-
orthodox haircuts and more concerned with why they are turning
out so many orthodox minds.**
Russell Baker, THE NEW YORK TIMES.

*What do you think should be the extent and limit
of school discipline?*

In what way is discipline a reciprocal responsibility?

*What concrete means can be taken between
student and administration to assure an atmosphere of respect?*

When the length of a boy's hair and the brevity
of a girl's skirt lose perspective in the eyes of school officials and
become evil in themselves, then the freedom of the individual
suffers, both because of his or her misuse of personal freedom
(defining it as the right to rebel) and because of the officials'
lack of understanding as to what the problem basically is. The
school gives the student no tools to constructively show that he or
she is unique, and does not want to be part of one great
sameness. Instead, it conditions the student to conformity, makes
it attractive, and then when the student sees what's happening
and attempts to express individuality by any means available—in
this case personal appearance (which is like a mute trying to
scream)—the school can't understand what's the matter with
these damn kids.

*What role does frustration play in freedom and
the school?*

**The young of America must be babysat and
policed for a longer period than ever before, so we conveniently
extend the concept of "youth." Our preferred means of keeping
them on ice is to keep them "usefully" in school. Unfortunately
the methods and tradition of American schooling work precisely
to *arrest* maturation. . . . But the schoolmarm attitude of the
elementary grades pervades the entire system, joining with
the convent-paternalism of the sectarian colleges. Thus, we
have corridor passes, censorship of hairdos and slacks, assigned**

lessons, grading, promotion, restrictions on political and social life.
Paul Goodman, "Moral Youth in an Immoral Society," THE YOUNG AMERICANS p. 18.

American schools teach students how to get marks, not how to deal with themselves and others. Lacking in most schools are courses in social sciences and elementary psychology, as well as training in self-discipline rather than authoritarianism and forced restriction.
A High School Senior.

How does lack of training in self-discipline become a drawback in understanding oneself and learning to use freedom?
What has been your experience in learning self-discipline?

Academic freedom is not license. It is not unlimited permissiveness. It is not the right to say anything one pleases at any old time to anybody. It is rather an intellectual open forum in which truth is trusted to take care of itself and state its own case, and error is constantly exposed to demands for proof, evidence and documentation. Freedom to investigate and report is necessary for any serious intellectual activity.

Freedom in a university classroom or in a kindergarten means, among other things, freedom to make mistakes. The possession of freedom to inquire does not guarantee the proper use of this right. Any freedom one enjoys might be abused. Therein lies one of the basic risks taken by free men, and never known by slaves.

Moreover there is no such thing as a little freedom. A man is either free or he is not free. Persons who do not see or accept this point often seek to legislate with their own system for limited kinds of permission for their fellows. Such legislators and such fellows may enjoy a variety of permissions. But they do not enjoy freedom.

All this is not to say that academic freedom is unqualified. It is qualified in many ways. In the world of ideas a

man must be prepared to stand his ground, defend his thesis and present evidence for his arguments when they come under fire. If he cannot do so, he is discredited and his effectiveness is diluted or destroyed, depending on the frequency or the gravity of his mistakes.

CATHOLIC MIND, April, 1967 p. 11.

"Academic freedom is not license." What does this mean? Give your own examples of how academic freedom can be used as license?

". . . there is no such thing as a little freedom." Is this true? And give reasons for your answer. ALWAYS give reasons for your answer.

Do you consider the last question a limit on your freedom as a student? What about having to give reasons for your answers—isn't that coercion, especially if you don't have any reasons, or don't especially feel like giving them?

What are some of the qualifications of academic freedom?

FREEDOM AND CHURCH

I go to church because my parents want me to. If they didn't make me, I probably would still go, but I can't be sure. I don't listen when I go now. I spend the time day-dreaming. I don't know if I'm insulting God but I don't think so, because I know my greatest belief is in God. What I want out of religion is to figure out a code by which I should live. I have none right now, and I can't just accept somebody else's. When I was little, everything came naturally. Now everything seems so complex. However, being 100 per cent secure is dead. When you are insecure, at least you are alive. I hope people will never become so narrow that they will start worshipping the thing that is created rather than the Creator. A lot of people do that right now by worshipping money. I don't want a lot of money. If you have a million dollars when you die, it doesn't make you a better person.

"The Separate World of Youth," THE YOUNG AMERICANS, p. 44.

What are your reasons for going to church?
". . . my greatest belief is in God." What is your
greatest belief in? Do you really believe in anything?
How are faith and freedom related?

If the thoughts of men and women become freer, and they begin to cast off old hang-ups and ignore moral taboos that have proved themselves the essence of immorality, then the organization which serves those men and women must also change, or be left as a quaint piece of memorabilia. The Christian Church has not only opted to throw aside the childish and the antiquated, but to take the forefront in moral growth, and act as an influence and an impetus for change among *all* men.

The "cult of stuffiness" in the Church is under fire from Msgr. George W. Casey, syndicated columnist, who would like to see us "give up a good deal of our stuffiness." He explains: "By this is meant that whole amazing establishment of vesture, head-dress, staffs, thrones, canopies, coats of arms, titles, genuflections, ring-kissing, deferences, processional order, protocol, etc. that characterizes official people in our Church and distinguishes them from anything else in the world save, perhaps, the British court at a time of coronation or maybe some small oriental court left over somewhere from the Middle Ages. It gets more space in the code of canon law than the rights of man, and it means more to some people than the gospel."
D. Herr, OVERVIEW, July 15, 1967.

What is meant by the "cult of stuffiness"?
How has stuffiness impaired the freedom not only of clerics
but of parishioners as well?
Do you think that all ritual should be done
away with?
Have some Christian symbols lost their meaning?
What are some of the symbols in the Church that should
be kept, and which still connote something rich to the Christian?
Is natural symbolism, such as water for cleansing
and white for purity, still valid today?

59

It is really not in the nature of things that the existence of authority makes the existence of freedom impossible, nor that the existence of freedom makes the existence of authority impossible. There is a large area between absolutism and anarchy, and there is no particular reason why anyone, whatever his position in the Church, should think that he must flee to one pole or the other.

J. L. McKenzie, "Christian Authority and Christian Obedience," DIRECTION Dec. 1966 p. 6.

"Be either hot or cold lest I vomit you" is a bad admonition to live under, particularly if you think it means imbalance, the denial of one necessity (authority) for another (freedom). If you reason things out, use your freedom and accept the responsibility of decision; you are not a mollycoddled, warm-milk momma's boy, as some might have you believe. And more important, you understand that life really isn't the good guys and the bad guys. There are simply some guys who just aren't sure.

For what causes and to what end would you be willing to go to extremes?

Is there anything you would be willing to die for?

FREEDOM AND FAITH

The faith of the child is spontaneous and unreflective. Naturally religious, the child seeks a protective environment in which he is surrounded by benign powers. He responds readily to the idea of heavenly forces that take him in their care. In the absence of serious challenge from without, the child is not compelled to think critically. He confuses myth with reality, illusion with genuine insight, and easily falls prey to superstition.

At the stage of adolescence, the critical faculties awaken. Prone to assert themselves as individuals, the young are often antagonistic to authority. On the other hand, their exuberant vitality, harnessed to a vigorous faith, and fired by zeal to transform the world by high idealism, can inspire great

A man's gotta be self-reliant, son. Ya don' see me askin
for, nor gettin, any privileges ah don' deserve.

feats for God. But the adolescent's faith has its defects. It is too often egotistical, assertive, more critical of others than of self. It needs the humiliation of experience in order to discover the value of suffering, sacrifice, submission. It has to lose some of its self-confidence before it can be properly receptive to the values others have to communicate.

A mature faith is one that overcomes the superficial enthusiasm of youth as well as the naive credulity of a child. Through harsh experience it has learned that evil persists and will persist, that man's ideals and labors, even when well intended, are shortsighted and ambiguous. Focused on God in mystery rather than in tangible values, such a faith is equipped to face tragedy, diminishment, suffering and death.

A. Dulles, S.J., "Faith Come of Age," AMERICA, August 5, 1967, p. 137.

". . . the critical faculties awaken." What does this have to do with faith?

What, for you, is a mature faith?

Can you have freedom without faith? Discuss.

FREEDOM AND RACE RELATIONS

The one hope is that as people of different colors mix with one another they will gradually lose the sense of difference that inhibits collaboration between them. There are some people—around the Mediterranean, for instance—who have never felt the sense of difference very keenly. There are others, like the West Indians, who have slowly come to find it a little less important than others do. There is the East Indian community in Holland, where the Dutch have made a better effort than anyone at integration.

THE ECONOMIST.

The inhibition caused by prejudice, which has been passed from parents to child almost as effectively as chromosomes, is a major drawback to personal freedom and growth in American youth. Racial discrimination causes harm not only to those being discriminated against, but maybe even more so to those discriminating, and particularly their children,

who are restrained by growing up in a segregated school and
living in what naturally appears to them as a segregated world.
So both the colored child in his ghetto *and* the white child
in his suburb suffer, because they are both cut off, and thereby
narrowed.
THE ECONOMIST.

Can you be free if you are prejudiced?

*Do you feel a sense of difference between yourself
and those of another color? If so, how does this hurt your
freedom?*

*Must you have no hate to be free? Or is that
a lie, concocted by some pious churchman?*

*"Boy, let me tell you something. Prejudice and
hate are as natural as the air you breathe. They've always been, and
by God, they always will be. That's the way we are, boy. The
good Lord made us that way."*

Is that the way we are? Is it?

Freedom is not license, it is growth. To ruin, to hurt,
to remove dignity where dignity is essential, these are not the
acts of a free man. They are negative and destructive, and
therefore we can rule out the possibility that they are products of
freedom. True freedom creates, never stagnates, and never
directs itself toward tearing down without a plan for rebuilding.

The Negro in America has been the kicking boy
for a lot of nice people weaned on the Washingtonian-Jeffersonian
manifestos of freedom. And while a man may think himself
free because he has freedom of press, of belief, of speech, etc.,
he is no more free than the man he persecutes, because the
man he persecutes puts the lie to his freedom, and says to him,
"You never had the freedom of heart; you have made yourself
suppliant to your fears and suspicions."

Every time a white man says "Nigger" to a
black man, all freedoms are lost—the white man has forfeited
his own dignity and right to respect. He has shown himself
shallow and insensitive—and more or less a bastard.

And likewise when a Negro throws a brick
through a window, protesting injustice, his freedom becomes
nothing because he has destroyed; he has used violence and

is no longer his own man, but the bootlicker of his anger and hatred.

The riot has become the means of communication of a small portion of the Negro population. Violence, frustration, the brick wall of desolation behind every back in a slum, these can be understood as symptomatic and the root causes of riots can be combated with more money for education and money for slum clearance, money to set up job opportunities, and money to combat prejudice with literature and films. But rioting, if integration and brotherhood of races (and thereby freedom for black and white) is ever to be realized and empathized with, cannot be condoned.

This will outrage those whites who believe that the civil rights legislation of recent years ought to have "satisfied" the negroes, and that these people are only proving themselves beastly ingrates by rioting in the streets. The fact is however that all this legislation has yet to produce real gains for ghetto negroes in employment, housing, or education; and while Southern negroes finally have the right to vote and eat grits in the local café, and a small percentage of them can even send their children to adequate schools, why should they be grateful for that? What gratitude is due a thief that steals your money, keeps it for a few generations and then grudgingly gives a little of it back under court order?
T. Wicker "The Deadliest Pollution," THE NEW YORK TIMES, July 13, 1967.

Try to get a copy of *Manchild in the Promised Land* by Claude Brown. And read it. You will then at least partially understand what Mr. Wicker is talking about. The results of denying personal freedom and dignity to a human being go too deep to measure. There's a short movie called *The Quiet One* about the Wiltwyck School for Boys. If you get a chance, see it. You will know then what anger is, and frustration for the slum dweller. You may find your own freedom infringed upon. Sorry.

FREEDOM AND POVERTY

But to stand in poverty, before God, and before one another, has one altogether unique advantage and reward.

It is the reward which a sense of reality always brings with it.
When one knows he is poor, not in the abstract, but in the flesh
and mind, in the soul, in his capacities, in his society, in his church,
he knows something extremely precious. He has touched things
as they are.

Indeed, in the constant thought of the Bible,
the poor man is man himself. As one veers away from the truth
of his poverty, he turns aside from God, from his brother,
from himself. He becomes alienated, a man obsessed by illusion,
unable to think or act or love, a man of false power and fearful
weakness. And on the contrary, when one is faithful to the truth
of his poverty, the needle's eye bursts apart, the narrow way
widens, the truth of existence opens up. One becomes fit
for the community, a meeting ground for the hope of man.

To refuse to give is to be condemned and deprived:
to isolation, to inertia, to acedia, to despair.
D. Berrigan, S.J. ACT, September, 1966 p. 10.

*Why is it that those who are voluntarily poor
have a much clearer vision of the basic and fundamental truths
of life?*

What does poverty in spirit mean?
How has the poor man "touched things as they are"?
*Why is refusal to give and share a limit on your
freedom?*

The rebel without a Utopia—without a cause
and without hope—knows only what he is against: he is unready
to assume responsibility for defining what he is for. He therefore
rejects not only the Utopias of his elders but also the
institutionalized expressions of those Utopias. He demands
the Happening—vivid, personal, immediate—and so becomes
essentially anarchic. Oriented to issues rather than ideology,
he is pragmatic. Indifferent to the past and without great hope
for his future, he will not readily claim a stake in the present.
Buell Gallagher, "Our Students Have No Utopia," THE
SATURDAY EVENING POST.

Meet the challenge: How do you intend to make society into something better?

What are you *for?*

We've talked about being free: a man or a woman who seeks the truth without hang-ups, without giving in to easy lies.

It means you face what is, and when there's something wrong with *what is,* you get angry, and you say Dammit, that is not the way it's gonna be for long, not if I can help it.

And then you try and help it. And it seems like it never ends.

Hey man—don't you know. It's all a game.

You're lying.

No man. I ain't lying. Really; it's all a game.

So you play the game, because you have to play the game to live. And you learn the rules, and the hundred different ways to play, and the thousand different games.

And you say Love, that's not a game.

Sure it's a game. You play it at a dance, in the back seat of a car, at school, with your parents and your friends. Love is the biggest game of all.

But suppose it's not a game. I mean suppose I refuse to play, suppose I really care about people and need them.

Then you get crucified.

Why?

Because that's the price you pay for the real thing.

**Pseudo love is love without the sweat. It's
damned scary to love somebody. They may leave you, hurt you,
betray you, kill you, etc.—those people whom you love.
Human life is very scary this way. Love is damned hard work—
and most people are too damned scared to do the work.**
Marion Powelson in THE VILLAGE VOICE, Dec. 15, 1966.

That's the way it is, folks. You can have your
love-ins and your up-tights. You can try drugs and aphrodisiacs,
jellybeans and Gibran. But that's the way it is. Love makes
demands. If you believe in peace, and flowers, and ring-around-
the-rosy, fine. But if you say you believe in love, and you are
afraid to sweat, really sweat for another person, then you are
either a liar or a fool.

In the next sections we want to speak about love.
There are excerpts from articles, from books, from poems,
from people's minds. And like the other sections, there are
questions. But the questions here are not so much for you to answer
as to think about. And please, think about them.

One more thing. It is the firm belief of the person
who wrote the questions and comments in this chapter, and
is now writing this introduction, that one must learn to love
deeply another human being before he can ever hope to love all
men, and God. And that the only sin there ever was, or ever
will be, is not caring.

LOVE AND SEX

**Boys and girls who have Dante for their pander
are more likely to make love with style, handsomely, than those
whose spiritual food is drawn from magazines and the films.**
Aldous Huxley, TEXTS AND PRETEXTS.

It's strange to think of love being made with
style, handsomely, yet with passion and satisfaction. Strange
because in America love is more often made with hunger,
clumsily in the back seat of a car or nervously in a borrowed
bedroom. The pander, the teacher, the guide, is not Dante, or
Tennyson, or the Lays of Courtly Love. It is the Hollywood

70

director, the paperback writer, the magazine editor, the advertising man, and they feel little hesitation when it comes to dipping their own sweet medias into the emotional and sexual drives of youth (and adults, for youth are merely the successors).

You accept French kissing as you accept rain, and if you don't stay in the clinch for at least fifteen minutes, then you might as well go home and have mommy dress you up in your little altar boy outfit and take you to see Aunt Harriet for some apple pie and ice cream. Make love like they make it in the movies and you'll get your kicks, but the odds are you won't get love, real affection, or happiness, which don't seem to be saleable commodities in American big business. Their substitutes, however, like pills and deodorants, keep the daughters of the illusion makers in low-cut dresses and mini-bras, and the sons in baby-blue convertibles. Face it. There are people selling you sex, and you're buying it, and I'm buying it, and we're all just one big sad bunch of sheep. Use sex as a game and you've loused up the one chance you have at becoming a part of another person. Use another person's body as an object, and you have denied yourself dignity, and taken away the tenderness of true physical loving. If you fake it, if you fall for the tricks, then you're going to be up-tight and guilty about the most beautiful and honest feeling that can be felt between two people.

Saying that sex is either good or bad is like saying that paint is one or the other. Paint splashed in hate on a synagogue door is bad. But that same paint in the hands of a Leonardo da Vinci is good through the centuries in the eyes of all who behold it. The difference is not in the pigment. The crux of the matter is in the way it is used.

You are learning that sex is natural. It is a God-given part of you. It is not to be denied. Whatever you do with it, it still will be there. You can throw it away and yourself with it, if you wish. Or you can learn to manage it, like the man or woman you aspire to be. Your sex life will be as good or as bad as you make it. No more, no less. Express it casually, as a simple biological hunger, and you go emotionally hungry as a person. Treat it as a reflex, and all you have is a simple release of tension. See it as the most intimate way in which two persons can merge their lives, and you find meaning that

is deep and lasting. One of the tragedies of taking sexual relations cheaply is that you miss out on the rich fulfillment that sex in a loving marriage brings.

Norman Vincent Peale puts this point succinctly when he writes:

"Sex in the right place and the right time with the right person under the right circumstances is a magnificent thing. But almost by definition this means sex under the seal and shield of marriage. Under any other circumstances it is likely to be clumsy, guilt-ridden and spiritually enervating . . . Sexual restraint does not mean deprivations; it means happiness in depth."

Evelyn Millis Duvall, WHY WAIT TILL MARRIAGE?, p. 31.

What does sex mean, now, this year?

". . . sex is natural." Is it? Is sex natural now that we are conditioned to certain mores? There is no doubt about it—sex used to be natural, and it used to be free and something beautiful. But that was a long time ago. What about now? Is it still beautiful, still natural? Or is it felt required, and caught up in rebellion?

". . . you go emotionally hungry as a person." What does it mean to be emotionally hungry? How does a view of sex as simply biological cause this? Have you ever felt this way?

What does the spiritual part have to do with sex?

LOVING ANOTHER

What do you do when you love one another? You do not have to *do* anything. You may be in love now, as you have been before, and as you will be again. But that does not mean that you must express all this warmth sexually. Just being drawn to another person is not sufficient reason for physical intimacy.

Love requires neither sex nor marriage for satisfaction. Unless you go in for serial polygamy, you do not rush to get married every time you are attracted to a member of the other sex. Hopping into bed with every individual you feel fond of would be ridiculous, if not downright immoral.

You keep yourself free to love and to be loved by many, many persons of both sexes, either married or unmarried, when you reserve your sex life for your marriage partner.

Of course you will love the one you marry. The one thing that will make this married love unique through the years is that it alone is expressed sexually. Saving sex for marriage gives you something very special to share with one another, which no one else can have. Into your married love, then, you can pour all your feelings as husband and wife, co-partners in building a marriage and family together.

Love then becomes a universal possibility to be developed widely without danger of harming your life plans or your beloved friends' family life. You can dare to love beyond marriage only when the threat of sexuality is removed from your non-marital associations.

Keeping sex for marriage protects you from others' exploitation. The British author J. B. Priestly reminds us that the lover is ready to give everything, all that is of value in his life. This makes a loving person vulnerable to "being used" by any unscrupulous person "on the make" unless sex is carefully regulated.

Premarital chastity safeguards you from deceiving yourself unwittingly. The danger is that you fall in love with someone who is not really there at all. You become bewitched by the magic of your own unconscious depths. Thus, you do not really see your beloved for what he or she actually is. When you feel lonely, rejected, or neglected (possibly with good cause), you are at the mercy of your own neurotic needs. You may convince yourself you are in love, when you are just licking your wounds. What you are calling "love" can be merely an escape from your problems.

You can avoid being trapped into going further in the intimate expression of your feelings by taking such practical safeguards as:
1. Becoming aware of your own lonely, rebellious, and love-hungry needs, and devising acceptable ways of getting back on an even keel emotionally without letting your feelings trick you into behavior you will regret later
2. Avoiding the fast workers and the loose company, whose moral standards are not your own
3. Keeping out of the compromising situations where you may not be able to cope with the consequences. Being alone together

in the privacy of a bedroom in a house, motel, or hotel, or the back seat of a car may be more temptation than either of you can manage

4. Recognizing that drinking and prolonged petting and erotic movies and risqué talk are all stage-setters for going further sexually than you may have intended

5. Respecting the urgency of the sex urge in yourself and others, enough to keep from being rushed pell-mell into going all the way until *you* decide you are ready

6. Participating in all sorts of activities while you are together —sports and music, trips and service projects, group fun and twosome discussions—so that you will not be caught in long periods of being together without anything to do

7. Being wary of going steady or getting engaged until you are really sure; then you can make plans for marriage when you are truly ready without the hazards of the too short or the too long engagement

8. Cultivating many ways of saying "I love you" without having to depend upon close physical intimacy for being or feeling loved

Evelyn Millis Duvall, WHY WAIT TILL MARRIAGE?, pp. 47–49.

Is physical intimacy necessarily the best way for two people in love to express that love?

How else can you show love?

How does love become a universal possibility for a person who is married? For a person who is not married?

Those who are most sensitive, most willing to give love, and give everything, are often the ones who are the most hurt, and they are most often hurt through sex.

What does it mean to love?

How do you love a girl who cannot love, and is bitter?

How external, how shallow is your understanding of other people, your feeling for their problems, from the terrible need to be admired and sought after, to bitterness and fear?

Has anyone ever shown you that love and sex are beautiful, and beautiful because they are both mysteries, and give meaning and dignity to a man and a woman, as well as great pleasure?

Have you ever been in love?

"I've passed my identity crisis and am ready to fall in love."

*Drawing by Whitney Darrow. © 1967 by THE NEW
YORKER MAGAZINE. Used by permission.*

Each of us knows that the only kind of life
that will ever make sense is the one in which the I-Thou
relationship is supreme. For this is the kind of love that is patient
and kind and not arrogant or rude. It does not insist on its
own way; it is not irritable or resentful; it does not rejoice
at wrong, but rejoices in the right. It bears all things. So faith,
hope, love abide, these three, but the greatest of these is love."
Evelyn Millis Duvall, WHY WAIT TILL MARRIAGE?, p. 82.

What is an I-Thou relationship?
How does it differ from an I-It relationship?
In his letters to a young poet, Rainer Maria Rilke
wrote, "Patience is everything. Everything." Why are patience
and kindness so important in love?
". . . but the greatest of these is love." Why?
Why should a man say that love is more important than faith
and hope?
How does love imply both faith and hope?

The simple fact is that you become what you are
to be in interaction with others. You find yourself in
communication with other human beings. It is the quality of
that communication that determines the kind of person you become.
One unfortunate result of premature sex experience
is that as soon as sex enters the relationship, other
person-to-person communication diminishes. One couple found
that they so anticipated their intimate moments alone together
at the end of the evening that they could not really enjoy a party,
or other couples, or even one another. Their relationship had
moved too fast to levels of intimacy that neither of them were
truly ready for. It was not surprising to find them breaking off
—as so often happens when sex relationships are not based upon
mutual knowledge, respect, and devotion.
Evelyn Millis Duvall, WHY WAIT TILL MARRIAGE?, pp. 82–83.

"The simple fact is that you become what you are to
be in interaction with others." And also in interaction with
yourself and your feelings, but why is interaction with others so
meaningful? Do the experiences and interactions you have with

others have an important effect on how you think, how you deal with yourself?

Things are changed when you kiss a girl for the first time, particularly if you've known her as a friend. Things are changed when you have the first intimacy with a girl. Why does person-to-person communication often diminish when sex enters the relationship? Does it always happen? When doesn't it?

Is devotion old-hat? If so, what took its place?

Family-minded persons see sex as an essential and positive force in marriage. They care about families as necessary for personal and social well-being. They usually have deep roots and ongoing loyalties that make it possible for them to maintain fairly strict codes of behavior. They find security not only in each other but in striving toward their dream of an orderly, secure world built solid by stable families. Standards that limit sexual relationships to marriage are clear-cut and workable for them. When sex is restricted to marriage, everyone knows what to expect of himself and others. Being married is a clear distinction about which there is no question. It combines permanence and security, love and sex in a generating relationship that establishes and safeguards a family through the years.
Evelyn Millis Duvall, WHY WAIT TILL MARRIAGE?, p. 92.

What are the things that make marital sex a richer experience than premarital sex?

What is the warmth of marriage and family? Do you want that, or is there something else? If so, what is it, and will you choose it?

Your relationship with your parents is a powerful factor in the kind of sex standards you maintain. If you have had a warm, close relationship with your father and mother through the years, you tend to look for warmth and understanding in your friends, and certainly in your life partner. If you have felt loved and appreciated, you very likely have confidence in yourself now, and therefore you don't have to rush off into impetuous affairs just to get a little loving in your life.

If you are able to talk things over at home, you find that problems do not loom so large nor get so tangled as when you just cannot get through to your parents with understanding.

If you find that you cannot seem to communicate with your parents as you once did, it is not a sign that anything is necessarily wrong with them, or with you. It may be simply that this is one way in which you are trying to emancipate yourself from your childish dependence upon your family.
Evelyn Millis Duvall, WHY WAIT TILL MARRIAGE?, p. 93.

How has your relationship with your parents affected you?

What does your relationship with your parents have to do with your sex life?

If the relationship has not been good, it is only natural that you want to break from it, and find some kind of love and affection, some kindness and willingness on the part of another to understand. What is the difficulty in finding that love and understanding elsewhere?

SEX AND AMERICA'S YOUTH

It seems to me that these are very difficult days to grow up in for a number of reasons, not only because of the pressure of our culture with all the mass media concern for selling products with as much sex and seduction as possible, but because of all the confusion we find among the adults with whom young people come in contact. At a recent gathering of fairly high-powered professional people, some notes were struck most persistently with regard to the question of what we should be saying to our young people.

"Permissiveness with affection"—as long as there is love anything goes. Well, I can't buy that. It seems to me that there is much more to love than just affection. I'd have to ask what *kind* of affection and *how much* permissiveness. It seems to me that to tell today's young people that permissiveness with affection is a new morality is only to confuse further an area that is certainly murky, to say the least.

Secondly, "if it's good for the relationship, it's good." Now this sounds usable; if it encourages and increases

79

trust and a feeling of unity and integrity, then whatever happens is all right—*if* it's good for the relationship. But I can't but help translate that kind of recommendation into almost any Saturday night date of the high school crowd or almost any fraternity party of the college crowd. I wonder just how much judgment in terms of what is going to be good for the relationship is brought to bear by persons in this kind of urgent situation.

Again, there has been a loud voice in recent years saying that sexual freedom should be the sixth freedom. I would suggest as a possible reply that part of that freedom must be responsibility, not only for others within the societal situation that is involved, but also responsibility for one's own best development and realization of one's human potential as an individual. I am convinced that freedom and responsibility go together. To openly advocate simple freedom is actually to ask for a kind of emotional unbuttoning without the kind of responsibility for the realization of the individual and social potential that people so desperately need.

You will recognize too another voice heard frequently: what we should be advocating today is honesty— an honest expression of feelings. It seems to me that there is a very healthy aspect to this that many of us can welcome. Anything that can shake us out of the hypocrisy in which many of us have been all too comfortable, anything that will make us face up honestly to the realities within ourselves and our social situation, is certainly to be encouraged.

But let's not be ridiculous about it! Let's recognize that honesty has to be in terms of behavior that is honest to the goals and values of the individual and of the society as well as to the impulses of the moment. Let's recognize that we have a challenge of integrity to the basic values that each of us shares as persons and as creatures in society.

A fifth opinion frequently voiced is the joyless hedonism of "let's express and express whether we enjoy it or not." It's the kind of individualism that says: "I am me and what I feel and what I want is the highest good." Yet everything we know about human nature indicates very clearly that life is more than sensuality; that it is realization, fulfillment, growth and development; that the sensual is a part of the human experience, surely, but only one part and it can't run the whole show.

A sixth opinion says: "Let's have the rule of love rather than law." Did it start with Augustine's, "Love God and

81

do as you please"? As I remember his history, he did as he pleased and then he loved God! But I see this and sense this as a very real kind of trap for our teenagers today. It sounds good and yet is based on a fallacy, for it fails to recognize that in every area of human life certain norms, certain rules are essential for survival. On the highway, on the waterfront, in a summer program, some kind of rules that will protect the silliest, the least mature, the most impulsive are imperative for the survival and the sanity of all the individuals involved. And I would suggest that the parked car or the drive-in movie are areas quite as filled with hazards as the curvy highway or the waterfront.

Next I want to mention the effects of playboy philosophy upon our culture. Now, I am not talking about all the wordy installments in *Playboy* magazine, but the playboy philosophy as it's put into flesh—the use of the woman as an animal, called a bunny. This, it seems to me, is a kind of philosophy that is blasphemous. To take a full half of the human race, the women out of which the next generation comes, and insist that they be used seductively as playthings, as the basis of titillation rather than respected as persons, is the ultimate blasphemy.

The last opinion is one that has come out of the marriage of psychiatry and religion in recent years. It says that the greatest sin against human well-being and mental health is the taboo. I suppose Freud started it all with his concern for the neurotic Viennese. But I wonder how Freud himself would feel today if he were suddenly to be plunked down in the middle of Chicago and see the nature of our neuroses. I wonder whether he would still feel that neuroses always come from constrictions and restrictions, from suppressions and repressions, or whether he would feel that you can get just as sick looking for some kind of reasonable expectations, some kind of sensible boundaries, and finding none.

Our young people are growing up at a time when they have more freedom, more opportunity for widespread experience and experimentation, at a time when it's extremely difficult for them to get any clear answer to some of the age-old arguments for proceeding further in their relationships with their companions. But if these youngsters—boys and girls alike— are to get any clear sense of their own identity, they must be given some kind of help to find their *own* answers to some of the pertinent challenges they are facing today. I would like to hold out six of these challenges for consideration.

First, the "everybody does it" pitch. We've heard this so often that a great many intelligent young people and a great many sophisticated, intelligent adults assume that just because we have so much talk about active sexuality—particularly in our youth culture and on our college campuses—this means everybody is doing it. Actually, we find that this is not the case; it never has been; in fact, there is no sexual revolution going on, genitally speaking. Whatever revolution there is, is still at the oral stage, literally. This is the picture that we get in study after study. The evidence right up to this last year indicates that there has been no increase in premarital sexual relations on the American college campus since Kinsey.

Secondly, our young people get altogether too little help in answering the objection that sex is natural. This a very intriguing one. It goes something like this: the good Lord wouldn't have made us into sexual creatures with sexual impulses unless he had wanted us to use them. Of course, the simplest answer is that man may share his sexuality with the other animals but that he had better know that he is more than just an animal. Everything we know about the development of a human being indicates that this dimension beyond the physical is what makes him human. The thing that keeps him human is his recognition of some kind of growth and control of his impulses, his appetites, his hungers which keeps them in line with his dreams, aspirations and self-concept. We recognize that our biggest task, as men and as women, is to establish our own masculinity or femininity in terms of our growing realization of what it means to be a person of one sex or the other, comfortably at home with members of both, comfortably at home in our own skin, aware enough of our sexual roles so that we may function effectively and comfortably and lovingly and with compassion towards members of both sexes wherever we meet them.

Even more compelling for many young people who have grown up in an age of affluence is the argument that "sex is fun" and therefore all right. When I am working with teenagers—hundreds of thousands of them every year—I am continually impressed with how little fun there is in the "messing around" that is so very prevalent among a good many who have to learn to their own sorrow that just the biological expression of an urge can be mighty disappointing and disillusioning.

83

Response to such a complex thing as the language-of-love-through-sex takes time to develop in an atmosphere of privacy, in an atmosphere of mutual trust, in an atmosphere of permanence, blessed by the Church, right according to law and the visions of families. This means within marriage.

The fourth argument that many of our young people are running into is: But if you are really in love, if you feel married, isn't it all right? And this is a hard one for many adults to answer because it sounds so terribly plausible—until you begin to get enough counseling experience with couples that have put this to the test. You begin to realize that after premarital sex experience the girl begins to press for marriage, especially if she becomes pregnant. She begins to press and nag and push for the date. At the same time, we find that the boy in the case begins to have some second thoughts, begins to wonder if she would do it with others, begins to realize that—after all—this wasn't so much. He often begins to have very real doubts that make it difficult for him to go through a marriage with any great enthusiasm.

Young people ask me very frequently: "Well, how can you tell how you'll feel after you've gone all the way?" I think if we are going to be honest we can tell them that sometimes they'll feel all right—not often, but it's possible. There isn't any way before you get into this kind of behavior that you can predict whether this will be good and whether you can live with it or not. Your own safeguard is to play it safe.

One of the most frequent comments or questions I get from young people both on college campuses and in high schools is the fifth argument, an old-hat one that I would have thought we had outgrown: But isn't sexual restraint bad for you mentally; doesn't something happen if you don't behave naturally? Well, I can say with complete candor that from all of the evidence there is not a shred of truth that physical, social, emotional or mental harm results from chastity. The response I get to such an answer is often, "Gosh! Why don't they tell us these things?" And why don't we? Why don't we come out with the same kind of clarity *for* chastity that the other side uses in applying pressures for the release of sexuality.

The last challenge I want to mention is: "What happens to your reputation if you don't?" My answer to that is very quick. It depends upon your reputation with whom: the playboy crowd, the acting-out crowd, the guys that are doing all the talking, the folks back home, the people you really care about, the people that you are going to be identified with? Reputation with whom?

And here is the place, I think, where the basic Christian message has a very real impact. We've tended all too frequently to allow a good many of our really fine young people to get themselves into a corner from which there is almost no way out unless Christians are there with a redemptive message. We've tended in our country to view these things all out of proportion. We say to the young person, as Kinsey did, "If you ever 'have,' you are over there with those who 'have'. Only the good guys and girls who never 'have', who are still virgins (at least technically), are over here, the good ones." In this method of counting, all those people over there that ever upon any occasion have stepped over the line, they are those who 'have' in the Kinsey kind of counting. It seems to me that we have done a very great disservice in our silence at this point. I am convinced that we who associate with the churches and the helping professions have let our whole generation of young people down because we have not spoken out forthrightly with the redemptive message of our religion.

We don't have to be stuck with our weakest moments. Yet too many of our really fine young people are. This is true of the girls that find themselves pregnant before marriage, and it's true with the young men who find themselves with a venereal infection, and it's true of a good many of our youngsters who have gotten into jams and have found out that our society, as a whole, is without the kind of caring for the person that goes beyond the symptom and the problem and that most Christians say they believe in.

Life is a flowing experience. Young people must realize that they are going to behave in marriage just about the way they did before they were married, and so is their partner. What we do and the way we come to terms with what we do, both in our strengths and our weaknesses, in a very real way determines step by step, day by day, situation by situation, what our future will be, the kind of person a man or woman will find as a partner, the kind of place he or she will find in society, and the kind of person one will become as an individual.

Fidelity in marriage is more than just a religious preachment. It is fundamental and essential for the basic security of the family. If we are going to want that much as most of our young people of both sexes do, then we have got to recognize that it's all part of the way we behave before marriage as well as after. We must recognize that life is built out of decisions and confrontations, based not on the most irresponsible, exploiting opinions but on a solid message of Christianity.

We have refused to bring in the basis of our Christian heritage, a redemptive message of love, the story of forgiveness, a recognition that each of us, with our human vulnerabilities and weaknesses, must come to terms with ourselves, with our sins, sorrows and mistakes. We must bring this message to bear so that we may assimilate all our experiences and grow out of them and through them.

Evelyn Duvall, "Sex and American Youth," LISTENING: CURRENT STUDIES IN DIALOGUE, Winter, 1967, pp. 38–43.

". . . as long as there is love, anything goes." Do you think that this is true, that there can be no wrong where there is love? And are all things done in love good? If love results in pain and suffering, does it necessarily mean that the love was wrong to begin with? How do some people use love as an excuse and a means of self-deception?

Before one decides what's good for a relationship, one must decide what that relationship is. How much thought do you think it is possible to give this in the back seat of a parked car at one o'clock in the morning with a member of the opposite sex sitting beside and/or all over you?

What does "sexual freedom" mean?

Does an "honest expression of feelings" mean just that, honesty and integrity in showing how you feel? Or is it used as merely a verbal ploy to get another to see things your way, do what you want them to and bingo! They are honest?

If you forsake involvement, you deny both the joy and the suffering. Why is sex without involvement, without deep love, empty and superficial? Do you think you can settle for just that?

Who was Alfie?

". . . everybody does it . . ." The classic answer to that used to be, "If everybody jumped off the Brooklyn Bridge, would you jump off the Brooklyn Bridge?" You might if it was a hot day, and again you might do other things if it was a hot day. But the facts are, everybody else isn't jumping

off the Brooklyn Bridge and everybody *else isn't engaging in physical sex activity, hot day or not. What does Dr. Duvall mean when she says, "There is no sexual revolution going on, genitally speaking"?*

Is sex fun? I mean is sex fun for you? *Is that the prime goal of sex—fun?*

Is the experience a happy one for the person with whom you are having sex? Did you ever ask that person? Do you care?

Why is emotional growth so important to an understanding of oneself and sex?

If there is anything that is sorely needed in the discussion of sexuality-morality, it is unquestionably the willingness to descend from our private pedestals of unchallengeable infallibility and re-enter the arena of amicable human discourse. The temptation to wax wise on sex is an alluring one, and in recent years veritable armies of sexual sages and sexperts have arisen.

Bernard Suran, "The Nature and Import of the Sexual Revolution," *LISTENING, Autumn, 1966, p. 183.*

How have studies such as the Kinsey Report *and* Human Sexual Response *affected attitudes toward sex in America?*

Do you think that they have done more harm than good?

Madison Avenue certainly deserves special recognition among the ranks of the omnipotents [over sexual behavior]. Consecrating almost every imaginable commodity with ingeniously varied but always erotic enticement, the advertising agencies bombard the babes of consumerland with a never ending barrage of sexual stimuli that invariably elicits the well-trained response at the cash register. I hesitate to explore the obvious, and I'm sure that anyone with a modicum of alertness must be well aware of the impact that the advertising industry has made on American sexual behavior.

Bernard Suran, "The Nature and Import of the Sexual Revolution," *LISTENING, Autumn, 1966, pp. 189–190.*

HOW YOUNG MEN INFLUENCE THE GIRLS
WHO LOVE THEM

Rare is the young man who is fully aware of the
important part he inevitably plays in the life of every girl with
whom he has a close relationship. He is indeed the exception
if he has any real understanding of his role in the evolution
by which a girl becomes a woman. For no woman is truly a
woman until a man has participated in and completed the process
that makes her one.

But because it is a process, the subtle, complex
evolution of a young girl into a woman occurs over a substantial
period of time and cannot be explained by any single act or any
single relationship. The French word for it, *epanouissement,*
which has no exact English translation, conveys the idea of
"becoming," and includes such nuances as growth, development,
unfolding, flowering and particularly, fulfillment. Often the
completion of a girl's coming of age will occur as a consequence
of her relationship with a young man who proves to be the man
in her life. But in maturing into womanhood, she will be
influenced by her involvements with all the men to whom she
becomes emotionally attached, including friends, teachers,
relatives, brothers and especially her father.

A girl's development is also influenced by her
associations with other women, and profoundly so by her relationship with her mother. And a boy's evolution into manhood is
similarly influenced by the girls and the women he chooses to like
or love. But I am concentrating here on the impact of men on
the life of every young girl with whom they share an emotional
bond. In my experience, men are generally unaware of the extent
of this impact—or unconcerned about it; as a result, their
behavior is all too often irresponsible. My hope is that in
sharpening their awareness of how a girl grows up, I may increase
both their concern and their sense of responsibility.

In the early years of her development, a girl must
strive to accomplish what one psychiatrist has called the four

tasks of adolescence. 1. She must separate herself from her parents—that is, become emotionally free of them without rejecting them. 2. She must establish a value system for herself, deciding on the moral principles and value judgments by which she will live. 3. She must choose her life goal, which will eventually enable her to be independent of her parent's support. 4. And finally, she must determine and accept her sexual role, which means discovering what it means to be a mature woman and accepting not only the joys but the responsibilities of her sexual nature.

Similar tasks must be accomplished by the adolescent boy. But our society has not made equal demands of boys and girls, especially in terms of their acceptance of the joys of sex as contrasted with the responsibilities. Boys have always been encouraged to develop their healthy drives toward sexual manhood, but little has been demanded of them in exercising responsibility. The opposite has been true for girls. Even in this day of the emancipated female, girls are hardly encouraged to express their sexual nature, but they are still expected to bear the burden of responsibility for all heterosexual relationships. In a changing society, however, as women increasingly share with men a healthy enjoyment of sex, so men should increasingly share the burden of its responsibilities.

There are two sides to responsibility, and they are equally important. One is responsibility to ourselves, and this includes the need to know what is right and healthy and nurturing *for us;* and then there is the responsibility for the other, the need to try to understand, to the limits of our ability, what may be best for the other person. In the latter sense, a young man can hardly be counted on to assume responsibility for the well-being of girls he dates if he lacks any real understanding of what happens to a girl as she slowly matures into womanhood. There is much that he needs to know.

He needs to know, for example, that she has in her unconscious an image of the ideal male that has been built up through her relationships with the men in her family and the men she has come to know up to this point in her life. She has also been influenced by our culture with its constant emphasis on sex —in newspapers, magazines, comic books, novels, television, plays, movies and, perhaps worst of all, the commercial advertising of exploiting sex for profit.

From this vast flow of experience the girl distills

her image of the ideal male. No matter what the character may be of a boy she meets, she tends to see her ideal image reflected in him because of her eagerness to find in the flesh the one male she seeks. Thus a first-love relationship is full of possibilities for misunderstanding, as when a girl who has been reared in a family dominated by a harsh father turns to a boy because he appears to be sensitive and thoughtful. If he is what he seems to be, he will reinforce her image of the ideal male. But if in reality he is a passive, selfish boy, sooner or later this will become apparent and disillusionment may force the girl to reject that image and accept harshness as the mark of a man.

We certainly cannot expect a young man, who may himself be relatively inexperienced in life, to comprehend fully the nature of a young girl's unconscious image of her ideal male. But it is not uncommon for a boy to sense the girl is looking for certain traits—firmness, perhaps, or sensitivity, or tenderness —and for him to assume these characteristics as a short cut to sexual conquest. If he succeeds in his strategy and then abandons the girl afterward, as often happens, it is because he is aware of —or unconcerned about—the extent of his irresponsibility. Apart from having consciously deceived the girl, thereby diminishing her trust in all men, he no doubt will have permanently altered for the worse her image of the ideal male.

A young man must therefore be prepared to face the fact that whether he likes it or not, and whether it is for better or for worse, a responsibility rests on his shoulders when he initiates a sexual relationship with a young and inexperienced girl. Often, however, he is in a poor position to assume such a heavy responsibility, since he, no less than the girl, is floundering in a sea of uncertainties and is himself not entirely sure of the ways in which love is related to sex.

Both the boy and the girl are seeking love and sex, but their needs are somewhat different. For the sake of clarifying the point, we can say the girl plays at sex, for which she is not ready, because fundamentally what she wants is love; and the boy plays at love, for which he is not ready, because what he wants is sex. We must understand that in reality both the boy and the girl seek love *and* sex, tenderness *and* passion, but that in the early years their drives are rarely synchronized. A girl usually has a greater need for a feeling of legitimacy about the relationship before she can give herself to a boy, a legitimacy rooted in her belief that the boy loves her and that she loves him, for it is this belief that frees her to express the sexual side of her nature. Boys rarely require such a belief to free themselves sexually, but they willingly play at love if this is necessary.

In truth, the girl as well as the boy "plays" at love. For real love in any form is composed of many elements, one of the most important of which is primacy of concern for the beloved one. And few are the girls or boys who have achieved emotional maturity to be able to identify the best interests of another person and put them ahead of their own.

There is, however, a crucial difference in how a boy and girl play at love. The boy can do so consciously; the girl cannot. In this sense, the boy can play at love as he would at any game, using strategy to win. The girl plays at love in a more profound and vulnerable way, since the person she must mislead—if she is to obtain what she wants—is herself. She has a need to *believe* in love, a need that the boy, in most cases, does not have.

If a young man does use love in this way, as a lure or a weapon, it is usually without his realizing the dangers in doing so, for this gives him the power to arouse the young girl's sexual nature. Whether he has the moral right to do so is, of course, the critical question. I am one of those who believe we need to develop much new knowledge on which to base new moralities adequate to the changing needs of a contemporary society. We do not know all the consequences of introducing a psychologically and emotionally immature girl to sexual stimulation. But we do know that in a large proportion of girls, sexual response does not appear spontaneously, as it apparently does in the male, but is learned at one time or another during the development into womanhood. And in this learning, the male plays the obvious lead.

We have always known this. Yet we do not shine in our ability to say to our sons: "Before you make love to a girl, you have an obligation to come to a deliberate decision in full awareness that you will be setting in motion powerful forces in that girl. If you are concerned about her as a human being, you must decide whether or not it is appropriate at her age and stage of development to learn sexual response. And you must decide whether she is ready for this. If you think she is, then you should acknowledge that it will certainly affect her life to some degree, and perhaps more profoundly than you can imagine. If you are not concerned about her as a human being, then consider what it will do to you—to your sense of yourself as a responsible human being, to your own character and development—to use her sexually for your temporary gratification. These decisions are your responsibility to make."

In my experience, few young men hear words of this kind. The plain fact is that we have lost the ability—or, more alarmingly, the willingness—to bring up sons with strength and self-confidence to assume major responsibility for setting standards and developing the moral values by which human beings must live. What lawyers term the "burden of proof" in establishing the rightness or wrongness of a sexual relationship has too long been placed entirely on the girl's shoulders.

Two years ago, for example, I attended a conference on the sexual behavior of college students, to find that those who had accepted invitations were for the most part deans and counselors at women's colleges. Why shouldn't there have been similar concern on the part of those who are occupied with the sexual behavior of college men? Doesn't it seem almost self-evident that in a society which proclaims the equality of sexes, men as well as women must come to grips with the question of sexual morality, and that men at least share the leadership in seeking its resolution?

Man cannot have his cake and eat it too. He cannot expect his eventual marriage to be the most enduring of all possible relationships if, prior to marriage, his relationships with women have been almost exclusively physical and transient. He cannot expect his wife to fulfill him in all ways if, before marrying her, he made little effort to learn about a woman's nature and needs.

Many young men (and women too, unfortunately) appear convinced that pleasurable sexual attraction is the most important single basis for entering marriage. In his autobiographical book, the writer Nelson Algren says: "I don't think of sex as just something that happens now and then. . . . Sex is a diffused feeling. It diffuses everything and only once in a while would it be called sex. Sex is diffused with love and affection, and I don't think you can make things like that happen. . . . It's got to be the big thing first.

I believe that every young man needs to know and to accept the fact that because he plays a crucial role in furthering a young woman's emotional maturity, he must accept also the responsibility that goes with it. He must understand that the sexual act for a woman tends to be the ultimate expression of what she feels about life and her belief in it, expressed through her love for and belief in the man with whom she chooses to live with the rest of her life. If she engages in sexual experience before she is mature enough, sex may become an end in itself— or the ability to enjoy sexual experience may be crippled forever —and her capacities for a deeper relationship may be arrested.

Young men must face these realities. We know that many young people today place their sexual lives beyond the reach of adult authority. But if they also place them beyond the reach of a better understanding of the place of sex in the life of man, they serve themselves and society poorly. We are changing and so is society. If we do nothing to direct the flow of change, negative and destructive forces will determine its course.

Of most profound importance to man and his well-being is his own sexuality and the use he makes of it. It underlies his most important relationship, and indeed pervades all his relationships in one way or another. The Reverend Kenneth Greet, of the Methodist Church in Great Britain, puts it this way: "The beginning of understanding is the recognition that sex is not primarily something we do, but something we are. We have been made male and female in order that we can come together in a unique kind of relationship. Marriage is the most vital form of it. The same act which secures, promotes and deepens that relationship can also produce a child. But there ought not to be any child until the relationship is there as the only fitting environment for it. This approach provides us with the right perspective for a fuller recognition of the immense importance and significance of sex. When we begin to accept it, it inevitably means death to the old double standard of morality. . . . It is also the means of quickening those elements of respect and responsibility which are a vital part of love, if it is to be worthy of the name."

In my sixties, as mother, grandmother and physician, and from the security of a long and fulfilling marriage, I would like to challenge the young men of this generation to ponder and answer for themselves the profound question: WHAT IS THE PURPOSE OF SEX?

The kinds of answers being given to this question have created the distorted images and concepts of sexuality for which my generation must accept full responsibility. But unfortunately we are not the ones who can resolve the situations.

94

You are. We can't tell you what to do—only that there is something of first importance to be done. Whether or not your generation does it is your choice. How you do it is your business. The standards of morality that must be set for the society in which you will rear your children are yours to define.

The truth about human sexuality as a great creative and re-creative force is yet to be acknowledged. The truth about the relationship of man to woman in the world of today as it turns into the world of tomorrow is yet to be discovered. Only from these two truths can be derived the Moralities that we must have if society is to survive as a community in which men and women can find fulfillment in enduring love.

Mary Stiechen Calderone M.D. "How Young Men Influence the Girls Who Love Them." Copyright © by McCall Corporation 1965 in REDBOOK, July, 1965.

What is this sense of "becoming" in a woman?
How great a part do men play in this process?
What are the four tasks of adolescence?
"But our society has not made equal demands of boys and girls . . ." Why is this called the double standard? How does it work?
What are the two sides to responsibility? Why are they both important?
How does the girl's image of the ideal man affect her relationships with boys?
In what way does a boy assuming certain characteristics of a short cut to sexual conquest hurt the girl who loves him?
A girl plays at sex when what she wants is love; a boy plays at love when what he wants is sex. Explain.
Why must a girl believe in what she wants?
How can the misuse of sex hurt both the boy and the girl in the relationship? How does it hurt the boy? The girl?
". . . sex is not primarily something we do, but something we are." What does this mean?
What is the purpose of sex?

Most people see the problem of love primarily as that of being loved, rather than that of loving, of one's capacity to love. Hence the problem to them is how to be loved, how to be lovable. In pursuit of this aim they follow several paths. One, which is especially used by men, is to be successful, to be as powerful and rich as the social margin of one's position permits. Another, used especially by women, is to make oneself attractive, by cultivating one's body, dress, etc. Other ways of making oneself attractive, used both by men and women, are to develop pleasant manners, interesting conversation, to be helpful, modest, inoffensive. Many of the ways to make oneself lovable are the same as those used to make oneself successful, "to win friends and influence people."

Erich Fromm, THE ART OF LOVING (Harper & Row), pp. 1–2.

In love, as in so many other things, we start at the wrong end. We try to make ourselves attractive, successful, lovable, all in a desperate hope to *be* loved. And if we only had thought to begin by loving, by learning how to love others, we would understand what love is—giving, without asking in return.

"It is this. And listen carefully. I meditated on love and reasoned it out. I realized what is wrong with us. Men fall in love for the first time. And what do they fall in love with?"

The boy's mouth was partly open and he did not answer.

"A woman," the old man said. "Without science, with nothing to go by, they undertake the most dangerous and sacred experience in God's earth. They fall in love with a woman. Is that correct, son?"

"Yeah," the boy said faintly.

"They start at the wrong end of love. They begin at the climax. Can you wonder it is so miserable? Do you know how men should love?"

The old man reached over and grasped the boy by the collar of his leather jacket. He gave him a gentle little shake and his green eyes gazed down unblinking and grave.

"Son, do you know how love should begin?"

The boy sat small and listening and still. Slowly

96

he shook his head. The old man leaned closer and whispered:
"A tree. A rock. A cloud." "
Carson McCullers, A TREE, A ROCK, A CLOUD.

The act of loving in itself is the most beautiful
human endeavor, more beautiful than cosmetics, groovy clothes,
and material success will ever make anyone over. There is an
integrity and a selfishness about a person who has learned to
love first. It's, I believe, the right order of things.

How does one learn to love?

HOW DO YOUNG WOMEN INFLUENCE YOUNG MEN?

**Sex implies gratification of lust urges and
also has to do with the goodness or badness of its being
experienced, with building character structure. And we all know
that character structure certainly determines how one relates to
other people and the world at large. So what goes on during the
young man's first sexual confrontations? Has he been encouraged
to think of his eroticism as a healthful and quite desirable thing?
Not on your life! He's a stranger in the dark.**

**And what does he discover in the girl with whom he
has his first, vital experiences? Honesty? Courage? Forthright-
ness? Oh, no. He finds, in a truly dreamcrazy way, that in being
with this girl in a seemingly innocent and profoundly intimate
exchange of Me and You, he is aware of another image. There is
almost another presence in the way she talks, words she uses,
gestures, responses, that have little to do with the real her.
And he gets the feeling that he is holding hands with or kissing
the girl's mother, or society or our culture or the entire female
and male faculty of his school. In other words, that she, too, has
been betrayed and manipulated and disengaged. . . .**

**Another thing the male discovers is that, unlike ice
cream or straight Scotch, sex is not sex alone. It cannot be
responded to directly. He finds that his sexuality must be directed
at the "right" girl, that is, one who will be best for him in his
life plans, acceptable to his parents' and friends' view of quality,**

and to that disgusting part of himself who says, always, "Play
the game, son." Then he discovers that some girls, but not more
than, say, 98 percent, use their sex to manipulate him, exact
rewards and deal out punishments. Is it any wonder that he ends
up just the weeniest bit unsure and troubled? Or lonely?
C. Brossard, "Who Says He's a Flop?", LOOK, January 10, 1967,
p. 23.

*". . . sex is not sex alone." What other aspects
has it taken on?*

*To what end do girls ("not more than, say,
98 percent") manipulate boys by means of sex? What are the
consequences?*

*Give some earmarks of "the game" played with
sex in American society.*

*Do you think the relationship between boys and
girls is the way it is presented in the above paragraphs? What
has been your experience of boy-girl relationships?*

LOVE AND DIVORCE

There were 340,000 divorce actions initiated by
wives last year in the U.S. . . . The American divorcee, compared
with her sisters in other climes, is a creature of unparalleled
privilege. Roman Catholic countries such as Spain and Italy
simply do not recognize divorce. Countries that do grant a second
chance, such as Japan and the Soviet Union, rarely award
alimony if the wife can tote a tray or wield a broom. In Sweden,
courts are so niggardly that a divorced woman with children
has a 1-in-3 chance of landing on the welfare rolls, while a wealthy
British divorcee may find herself forced to pay $15,000 a year
in alimony to her husband. . . . U.S. courts customarily cushion
the ride by awarding the divorcee custody of the children, the
home, and at least one-third of the husband's annual earnings.
And increasing equality in employment and education allows
her to slip into her old career—or fashion a new one—with
relative ease. . . .

The U.S. divorce barometer is not on the rise; in
fact, it has hovered around the 400,000-a-year level since World
War II. Nor is there a "soaring" teen-age divorce rate—figures

show that while the rate is rising, the rise is not very substantial. Instead, and far more significant, there is what one New York divorce lawyer calls an "epidemic" of breakups among solid, middle-class marriages of long duration. Nearly 40% of all ruptured marriages today have lasted ten years or more and 13% have survived more than twenty years. The median age of the U.S.'s 2 million divorcees is now 45. Furthermore, belying the myth that progeny preserves marriages, some 60% (vs. 42% in 1948) of today's divorced women have children under 18 at the time of the breakup.

The Children of Divorced Parents. Children, of course, are perhaps the most serious business of divorce. The struggles over their custody, visitation rights, the psychological gap left by one missing parent, the agony of seeing their lives dislocated, the possibility of less money to support them, all these problems rack both mother and father. But the mother, who generally wins custody, bears the greater load. "It's awfully difficult to bring up children," says one New York divorcee with a 7-year-old son. "I try to provide the warmth and the understanding of a mother, the discipline and companionship of a father, and not get irritable all the time. That's really it, you're always so irritable." . . . Not too long ago it was usually assumed that the child of divorce was destined for the police station or the psychiatrist's office. Clearly some end up there. Yet almost every serious scientific investigation of such children has concluded that most turn out emotionally sounder than those living in the twilight of a discordant marriage. Breaking up, rather than staying together "for the sake of the children," is frequently the more merciful course. . . . If it is true that such children often grow up surprisingly unscarred, they nevertheless seem to inherit a more flexible code toward life. Columbia sociologist William Goode has discovered in his classic study of 425 formerly married women in Detroit that divorce breeds divorce. More than half of his subjects, he found, were the offspring of broken marriages; in addition, the percentage of those whose own children eventually chose divorce was noticeably higher than the norm. A recent study of 321 students by University of Iowa sociologist Ira L. Reiss has uncovered a tangential trend: the daughters of divorced parents were 15% more likely to accept premarital intercourse than those of intact marriages. . . .

Solutions Offered. "It's too easy to fall into marriage and too hard to get out. Many mismatched people therefore remain together, which is uncivilized. The thing should be reversed. It should be more difficult to get married than divorced" (says divorcee Claude Cavitt-Sharp of Houston). Many marital experts agree. New York attorney Richard Wels would make marriage harder to enter into by establishing a mandatory, 30-day "cooling-off" period before a license could be issued. Sociologist Mervyn Gadwallader would make divorce easier to obtain by treating marriage as a flexible contract—perhaps for one or two years' duration—with periodic options to renew. And anthropologist Margaret Mead would mesh both approaches by having marriage in two forms: the first, easily dissoluble, would not include the bearing of children; the second would be explicitly directed toward the founding of a family and would thus be more difficult to initiate. Such extreme measures are hardly practical, nor do they cut to the crux of the problem. Monogamy might well work better if the American woman reduced her "great expectations" at approaching it. The notion that the pursuit of happiness is the goal of marriage is strictly a contemporary one. Other societies have constructed lasting and apparently successful marriages on far more mundane foundations, such as maintaining social status or uniting family bank accounts. It would be insidious, of course, to suggest that Americans should marry other than for love. But the U.S. divorce fever might well abate if more couples considered the concept of "limited expectations." All such analysis, however, is so much wishful thinking. Today's woman clearly insists upon a reasonably happy life and is increasingly unwilling to commit herself to a marriage that denies it.

"The Divorced Woman—American Style," NEWSWEEK, Feb. 13, 1967, pp. 64–70. Copyright, Newsweek, Inc., February, 1967.

How has a change in the attitude of American women entering marriage increased the divorce rate in this country?

What do you think of parents staying together solely for the sake of the children? Is it better than getting a divorce and leaving the child with one parent?

Do you think it should be made more difficult to get married?

How effective do you think Richard Wels' suggestion would be?

What does the writer mean when he suggests going into a marriage with "limited expectations"?

It is Saturday evening.
You take a walk.
The sun is taking its
last look around before it
disappears and gives way to
neon lights, illuminated
billboards, racing homebound
cars and tired people
who are tired of being busy
and who are busy about
thinking up things to do which
will make them forget
what made them tired. It's a
poor way to live and be
happy. It's phony and ungodly
and unnatural.

The rich blame the poor for being poor;
the poor blame the rich for taking it all. The rich put the poor on
    relief.
The aged poor, the sick poor, the decent poor, are exploited by
the voluntary poor who refuse to earn their bread by their own
    sweat.
So they cry out, "Give me my rights," and God whispers,
"Fulfill your obligations." And a bumper sticker shouts,
"Stamp out poverty! Work!"

Let's not close
our eyes.
We see it. Poverty.
Sickness. Want.
Unemployment.
Old Age.
Somehow all these
programs for the poor
are not enough.
The poverty isn't
just around us.
It's inside. I am poor.
Poor and sick and
lonely and old in sin.
I want.

I am unemployed
with the love that
could cure so much
of this.
I "love" myself
so much that
I really *don't* love.
What IS rich and poor?
Who IS rich and poor?

People seek money and grow rich. They worship their
bodies and wealth as their god. People lack money and health
and curse God. Christ counseled voluntary poverty through love.
Ambition and greed nailed him to a cross. Those in religious orders
live in poverty and penance. People laugh and call them irrelevant.
"They don't know what they are missing." Maybe it's because
they do know what they are missing, because they
really do love Christ, because they don't worship their bodies
or money that they are rich in happiness.

It's really very simple.
You can work like mad and paint up
poor people's houses and be
a counselor in a camp for deprived
boys, and feed the hungry bums,
and clothe the naked in India, and
teach retarded children and join
the poverty bandwagon
and all that. But . . .
if you don't have charity, you are
like a rusty bell; nothing but a
muddled sound. It's phony and
unnatural and ungodly.

You are poor. I am poor.
Love brings meaning and richness
to life and dissolves selfishness
and greed. Christian commitment is
a poverty program that starts
in the heart. Your heart and mine.
Solve your poverty and you will
help the poor. Our new
bumper sticker reads:
"Stamp out poverty! Love!"

103

The first rule, always, is to hang loose.

Relax your jaw, chew gum, and let the fist become a hand again. Don't get up-tight. It cramps your style.

Sure there are problems. This book is about problems. So what. That doesn't mean it all has to weigh on you like a fat monkey. Ease up. Give yourself a chance to think. Get a clear vision of things. Think positive. Think about the good stuff and the good times and how it feels to be happy— and sort of new. And how it feels to love, and be loved by the people who count, because they are free and unafraid.

No lies to tell, no masks, no put-ons, no royal fakes. You're doing your thing. You're being what you know inside you were meant to be. And the emptiness inside is all filled up. With caring. And understanding.

And that's what we're talking about here! Finding out about happiness. About hope.

About our lives.

IT'S A BEAUTIFUL WORLD

I Feel Drunk All the Time

"Jesus it's beautiful!
Great Mother of big apples it is a pretty
World!

You're a bastard Mr. Death
And I wish you didn't have no look-in here.

I don't know how the rest of you feel,
But I feel drunk all the time.

And I wish to hell we didn't have to die.

O you're a merry bastard Mr. Death
And I wish you didn't have no hand in this game

107

Because it's too damn beautiful for anybody to die."
Kenneth Patchen SELECTED POEMS New Direction Book.

On the sidewalks are people like "Sam," 23, blonde, exquisitely featured, the daughter of a Louisiana physician. She "couldn't believe what people said," back home. Now she has found "all the things I've secretly wished for," including "smiling at people on the street and having them smile back." And there is Joan A., 18, a dropout because, she says, college teaches useless facts and skills—"not what we want—which is wisdom, to learn to live with ourselves and others." At the moment, the hippie creed tells Joan that love is the supreme value, freedom its necessary condition, helping others its expression, and mind-expanding experiences its inspiration.
YOUTH QUAKE, p. 45.

Does getting all the things you've "secretly wished for" produce happiness?
"Give, and it shall be given unto you is still the truth about life." (D. H. Lawrence)
Hippies do *help others. And at least up till now they seem quite happy doing it. Helping others can be learned a lot quicker today from a good hippie than a "good" Christian. What does giving have to do with happiness?*
Have you ever taught a child anything?
That's giving.

What is fulfillment? A careful analysis of experience suggests that fulfillment is to be equated with personal adequacy. A person's quest for fulfillment, then, is actually his search for personal adequacy. The longing for fulfillment is a cry to be a whole person—to be complete psychologically. On close examination, fulfillment reveals a subjective as well as an objective aspect. Subjectively, fulfillment is a person's self-evaluative experience that he is someone who is self-accepting, self-possessed, reasonably self-confident—a whole person. Objectively, it is the sum of the mature abilities, wholesomely, progressively realized, that constitute a complete person. It refers to

**the actualization of one's potential to become a whole, mature
human being—something innate in every human being.**
*Sr. M. O'Keefe, S.S.N.D. and Fr. J. J. Evoy, S.J. "Personal Fulfillment
in Man and Woman," AMERICA, Nov. 12, 1966 p. 582.*

The problem with a lot of things written about
happiness and how to achieve it is the abstract and psychological
language used. You can understand it all right, but it just
doesn't hit, and if it *does* hit, the wound is seldom more than
superficial.

And it's really too bad, because these are the
people who have the facts. Just look at the word "fulfillment."
There used to be a commercial for Graham Crackers (the only
way to eat Graham Crackers, by the way, is to dunk them in
milk until they're just about to break off, then whip them up into
your mouth) on TV, and it said you could get rid of that "hollow
feeling" by chomping on these things for a while. It didn't work.
No sir. The only thing to make you feel good, and complete,
ever—was happiness and peace. And you get happiness and
peace by living up to what you always felt you were inside. By
not letting yourself down. By loving, and caring.

What about this word "self-evaluative experience"?
You find out what you're capable of by going into yourself, looking under the rug inside you, and into the closets, and understanding where it's at—for you. Then you go out and try—and
you hope. And that's all. That's all a person can do who decides
to play it straight. Try like hell—and then hope.

Like the man says: You gotta know who you are
to be yourself. Then have the guts to be it.

**Some people seek fulfillment in sexual experiences;
some seek it in pleasures and thrills of other types. Younger
individuals, particularly, look for it in dedicated commitment to
the poor and needy at home and in other lands, or in new and
different sense experiences, often through the mediation of some
type of drug or narcotic. Still others see wealth as holding the
key to fulfillment, and slavishly pursue riches. Many a person is
persuaded that fulfillment is to be found in one or more creative
expressions of his own personality or in some achievement worthy
of his efforts. Those who look for personal fulfillment in being**

110

respected and well liked by important people understandably give a priority to status symbols; these persons often are strongly motivated toward winning social prominence or business advancement. A husband hungering for fulfillment may in some instances require the most beautiful and lavishly dressed wife in his social group; her very appearance would bespeak his success. A number of persons set their sights on the attainment of professional or academic degrees. Finally, the attempt to find fulfillment in just one more marriage has become a commonplace.

But clinical observation of many of such fulfillment seekers reveals their frustrating disappointment after they have achieved these longed-for objectives. Whatever satisfaction their achievements may have brought, they clearly failed to give the desired fulfillment. For these persons have been looking for it in the wrong places. The longing for fulfillment, like hunger, is something real and demands to be alleviated. But, unlike hunger, it does not reveal the identity of that which can alleviate it. It should be pointed out, moreover, that those with the greatest hunger for fulfillment receive the least amount of it. This is another instance of the "haves" receiving far more than the "have nots."

There is a psychological explanation for the fact that persons most preoccupied with the quest for fulfillment receive the least of it. It is an emptiness that motivates the "have nots" to seek fulfillment. Regardless of what it might prove to others, no accomplishment can convince them of their own personal adequacy, precisely because they are so empty. For them, the performance they achieve coexists with their emptiness and is not a denial of it. Hence, all such achievements are but transitory gratifications, failing completely to produce the promised fulfillment and ending up in disappointment.

There is a lesson to be learned from the youngster who rides daringly on his bicycle, calling to his mother: "Look, Mom, no hands." Her admiring attention is rewarding to him in direct proportion to his knowledge that she loves him. Only if he is sure of her unqualified acceptance of him as a person is her approval of his performance deeply satisfying. While achievements of various kinds, in and of themselves, are rewarding, they need not be fulfilling. Though achievements cannot produce fulfillment in a person who is empty, to the extent that fulfillment is already present, they add to one's personal enrichment. This accounts for the fact that those gain most enrichment from their achievements who have least need of it.

Adequacy ought never to be confused with competency. A person may be capable of significant achievements in a number of areas and at the same time be lacking in personal adequacy. The tragic fact is that achievements alone, regardless of their caliber and number, invariably fail to fulfill a person.

Since achievements, of themselves, do not produce fulfillment, what does produce it? Fulfillment flows from the warm, interpersonal relationships in which one is loved by and loves the persons who really count in his life. An individual who has genuinely loved and been loved from infancy by parents and other important members of his environment experiences basic fulfillment. In a word, human love is the primary source of personal fulfillment.

At this point, it is necessary to distinguish clearly between love, affection and the expressions of affection. Love, in and of itself, is a going-out to another person in terms of placing a real value on that person and wanting the good of that person for his or her own sake. And though presumably an angel could have such love without any associated affection, a human being could not. The affective component made up of the feelings and emotional states is always present in human love. So while affection does not constitute the essence of human love, it is nevertheless inseparably linked to it. Any communication of one's real care for another person, regardless of its manifest warmth, is a true expression of affection; and any demonstration of personal feelings for another, no matter how ardent, that does not stem from love is not affection. It ought to be called by some other name.

The person who has not loved and been loved is an empty person. And because he is empty, he lacks the capacity to receive genuine love. Since he cannot accept real love from others in such a way that he becomes personally ennobled by it, he must twist it into one more selfish achievement or possession. As a miser, the empty person takes what is given and hoards it for himself. He cannot love, since love is a giving of self. As a psychological zero, he has nothing of self to give. So at best, any giving that he does must be in terms of things. He gives things in order to buy or to obligate, but never to benefit the other person. He is not personally enriched by giving to others.

What, then, is the relationship of fulfillment (personal adequacy) to maturity? Maturity is adequacy in action; it is the total expression of one's ability *to be*. It is the observable expressions of the successively maturing "abilities to be" that constitute a person's maturity. The chronologically adult person is mature as a person when he exercises all his abilities to be what he ought to be—a whole, adult person. The adequate person, and only the adequate person, is a mature person.

Many persons, unfortunately, look for fulfillment in the right place but in the wrong way. Sensing that fulfillment is to be found in persons rather than things, they attempt to form real relationships with people. Since however, they are incapable of love, they go "affection hunting." With a peculiar kind of cannibalism, they strive to fill themselves by devouring others psychologically. This they do by using them sexually, socially or in some other self-seeking way. Since personal fulfillment is to be found only in the giving and receiving of self, such draining of others removes any possibility of fulfillment. Affection hunters destroy the freedom essential to genuine love by selfishly obligating the other person to unreasonable terms set in jealous possessiveness. Regrettably, in their hunger for fulfillment, these persons fail to understand that "thing-izing" and so using another human being rob the relationship of all its potential for fulfillment. For the person who is empty, however, there is the possibility of some amount of fulfillment. It can happen precisely to the extent that he makes himself able to respectfully receive whatever genuine love and affection are offered to him by others. To this extent, his emptiness is filled. But ordinarily, persons who are completely empty are in need of some type of professional help in order to move toward such fulfillment.

Sr. M. O'Keefe, S.S.N.D. and Fr. J. J. Evoy, S.J., "Personal Fulfillment in Man and Woman," AMERICA, Nov. 12, 1966.

"It is an emptiness that motivates the 'have nots' to seek fulfillment." Does this mean that if you are concerned with fulfilling your potential you are automatically empty? What does it mean?

Why is acceptance as a person so necessary to be deeply satisfied?

"The tragic fact is that achievements alone . . . invariably fail to fulfill a person." Why?

". . . human love is the primary source of personal fulfillment." How, if at all, have you experienced this?

If I worship you, Lord, will you give me peace of mind?

... and fame,
and success in business?

... and give a personal,
written guarantee of immortality
for me and my family?

Oh—I must worship you
"because you are God"?

What kind of a deal is that?

"The person who has not loved and been loved is an empty person." Explain why love is totally inseparable from happiness.

What is "thing-izing"? How does it destroy the possibility of personal fulfillment and happiness?

How does an adequate, mature woman *differ from a* female?

How does an adequate, mature man *differ from a* male?

What role does personal fulfillment play in a person's happiness?

I figure my ideal is someone who is really happy in what he is doing. When I say "really" I mean to say intrinsically, deep down, because that's where it counts.

Now this guy who is happy can be anything. A truck driver, a politician, a teacher—anything. And he's happy because he's doing what he has to do because he wants to do it, and not merely because he *has* to do it.

I suppose this guy must be living up to his potential and all that, but that's really part of it. I doubt seriously a man could be happy knowing he could be doing something on another plane which he could do better. Someone like that more than likely would be discontent—a characteristic which does *not* breed happiness.

And this word happiness is not exactly right either. It sort of connotes walking around with a stupid grin on your face all day. There is pain and sorrow in life, but when a man is fulfilled in what he is doing, the pain and the sorrow take on a perspective essentially the same as joy and good times.

You see there's a core inside all of us, and if it's rotted because of discontent, because of fear to know ourselves, the taste of our lives is bad when we are alone and thinking. But if the core is full and rich, the taste of our lives is sweet in moments of solitude. When all shame is stripped, my ideal knows that it was worth it to be born, because he is filled up inside with the acceptance of himself and the dignity of his person.

A High School Senior.

116

"And he's happy because he's doing what he has to do because he wants to do it . . ." Is there anyone you know who has been able to do this? Are they happy?

". . . the pain and the sorrow take on a perspective essentially the same as joy and good times." What does this mean? Do you believe fulfillment can do this?

How do you feel about your life when you are alone, and thinking? Do you think about it much?

Was it worth it to be born?

HAPPINESS AND TEILHARD DE CHARDIN

The individual, if he is to fulfill and preserve himself, must strive to break down every barrier that prevents separate beings from uniting. His is the exaltation, not of egotistical autonomy but of communion with all others! Essentially the Universe is narrowing to a centre, like the successive layers of a cone: it is *convergent* in structure.
Teilhard de Chardin, THE FUTURE OF MAN (Harper & Row), p. 46.

Why is communion with others so important for the happiness of all men?

In what way are happiness and hope shown to be part of the same expression in Teilhard's words?

This is the gift of Teilhard: he has taught us to look long at the world, to love it . . . I sometimes encounter men who ask me (and I detect a kind of fear in their voices): "Are not men today growing more and more presumptuous? God will surely not bear much longer with our insolence: our space launchings, our invasion of the atom . . ." The implication of such words is instructive. It has something to do with the old notion of a jealous God, determined not to be outdone by man. But can such an attitude be authentic in a God who is our Father? Surely His joy is great as His sons advance with more confidence into the universe.

Indeed the day will come when men will stand upon what they thought was the most distant star; from there they will move forward into millions of new worlds. On that

What if when we get there it isn't any better?

day our idea of God will be somewhat less puny and inadequate. All blessings on Chardin, who has invited us to walk, without fear or second thoughts, into the heart of matter itself!
JESUIT MISSIONS March 1966, p. 8.

". . . to walk, without fear or second thoughts, into the heart of matter itself!" In what way does understanding create hope, rather than exclude it?

Why is hope necessary for happiness?

What is the hope presented by Teilhard?

PERSONAL FULFILLMENT

I just can't make ideals and realities part of the same story. I mean I have an idea of how I should act with a girl, but the whole thing gets all fouled up when the two of you are sitting there making out. Or when you know damn well you're supposed to give—for to give is to love—and when the times comes you hold your breath till the situation is past, and then gasp and say "Too bad about that." And I see the ideals of the people who have lived longer than I have, and I hear their sweet words and their mellow aphorisms but know too well their less-than-virtuous actions to believe. And so I am suspicious. Of them. Of myself. Of others. And it becomes hard to believe sometimes. To believe even what you think is the truth, what you feel inside is the real thing. Now I'm not saying I don't believe anything. That's ridiculous. But it becomes harder to say the *ideal* is right when too, too many believe that the reality, practical and material and possibly shallow, is right.

I think to be a Christian man, a guy has to decide if he's going to play it the way he knows it should be played, or play it the way the guy next to him is playing it—and making out just fine. I figure that's where Jesus comes in, with the strength to make the right decision, and someone to look at who made it by playing it straight.

A High School Senior.

What is the hope which Christ offers?

Is it real?

119

"By reason of his union with Christ . . . man attains to a new fulfillment of himself . . . This is the highest goal of personal development."

"It is a question of building a world where every man, no matter what his race, religion or nationality, can live a fully human life, freed from servitude imposed on him by other men or by natural forces . . . a world where freedom is not an empty word and where the poor man Lazarus can sit down at the same table with the rich man."

"Far from being the ultimate measure of all things, man can only realize himself by reaching beyond himself. As Paschal has said so well: 'Man infinitely surpasses man.' "

"Man must meet man, nation meet nation, as brothers and sisters, as children of God. In this mutual understanding, and friendship, in this sacred communion, we must also begin to build the common future of the human race."

"The superfluous wealth of rich countries must be placed at the service of poor nations. The rule which up to now held good for the benefit of those nearest to us must today be applied to all the needy of this world."

"Among the less human conditions of life we must mention the lack of material necessities for the poor and the moral deficiencies of those who are mutilated by selfishness."

"The new name for peace is development."
Pope Paul VI, ON THE DEVELOPMENT OF PEOPLES.

"By reason of his union with Christ . . ." Do you think man can reach his highest fulfillment without development of his spiritual nature? Do you think Christ is essential to fulfillment? What factor is common to all men who reach the highest goal of their own personal development? What do you see as the highest goal?

Can a man be spiritually barren and yet, as a person, quite happy?

What of humanism—is it possible to have real interpersonal relationships solely on a human and material basis?

In what way is development the practical application of hope for peace and happiness for all men?

Why aren't we happy when we've got so much?

HOPE FOR THE HANDICAPPED

The Pope has written a letter: *On the Development of Peoples.*

A beautiful, perilous vision of man in history! Almost as though one were to say, mankind, like a truncated body, can grow new limbs in response to new needs.

But it is precisely here that the biological analogy breaks down, and the spiritual reality bursts through. That is to say—

Of course an amputee cannot grow new limbs, no matter how urgent his needs or how fervent his longings.

And—of course mankind can grow into new forms of community, new international agreements, new alternatives to violence, new expressions of faith and love, new heights of altruism—all in accord with the new demands which his times place on him.

Hope for man! This is the deepest current which invigorates the letter of Paul. Man can still make it! The Pope believes it with all his heart, and he adds: Here are some of the practical things to be done, if hope is to win out . . .

Share your goods. Have compassion. Make peace with your enemies. Grant others breathing space. Stop wasting the earth. Unlearn avarice and selfishness.

Men need hope most when despair seems most reasonable. That is why this letter is good news. Despair is seductive and rank and pollutes the atmosphere. We have been hearing so much bad news about ourselves, for so long, we have come almost to believe it—to live by it, to fear it, to arm for its sake, to die of it.

We have grown less and less able to grow limbs for reducing distances, limbs for drawing other lives to our own, limbs for building and planning and loving and dancing and making music and . . . but where does man stop, if he is man, if he has grown up, if his body is whole?

He never does, of course. He is his own good news. He is discharged from the hospital. He is risen.

D. Berrigan, S.J. "Hope for the Handicapped" JESUIT MISSIONS March, 1966.

I   *How have you been handicapped?*

Good Lord! It's a flower!

What do you see now as the beautiful things, the things that will bring happiness?

Do you believe He is risen?

What hope is there if He has not?

THE IMPOSSIBLE DREAM

I know, I know, man will answer. I have tested the scriptures too. But when I want to say "I believe," I can only say "I want to believe." Want to—do you hear? I want to believe like a shepherd or a king—or a sinner. But where in the world is He? No one is there. The whole world is like an empty stage set, an empty crèche. The center, the poet says, falls apart. No one stands there. No one is born. So the kings pack up their gifts and go off wearily, the shepherds melt back into the crowd, the children grow distracted and run off. The faithful go elsewhere—some in faith, some in regret.

I hope we never lose hope. That would be the tragedy. That would be the drought; all the wells and water-sheds of the world down to dry rock. Every man his own policeman and his neighbor's enemy, every man building his bomb and guarding his bomb shelter, armed to the teeth. Such a world, I hope, Christ would indeed flee . . .

I hope all bombs dissolve into butter for hungry men.

I hope (imagine!) this year—no one dies! No one dies. I mean, in the final glacial death—into hopelessness, into violence, into power that is empty of conscience, into dread and nausea and inaction and egoism and base fear.

Sing it out—all the graveyards gone!

Sing it out—enough light to go by!

Sing it out—enough brothers to live for!

Sing it out, Jesus, Son of Man—we can make it!

D. Berrigan, S.J. "Where in the World Is He?" JESUIT MISSIONS.

What is the message of hope expressed here by Daniel Berrigan?

What hope do you envision for the happiness of man?

124

The longer I live, the more I feel that true repose consists in "renouncing" one's own self, by which I mean making up one's mind to admit that there is no importance whatever in being "happy" or "unhappy" in the usual meaning of the words. Personal success or personal satisfaction are not worth another thought if one does achieve them, or worth worrying about if they evade one or are slow in coming. All that is really worthwhile is action—faithful action, for the world, and in God. Before one can see that and live by it, there is a sort of threshold to cross, or a reversal to be made in what appears to be man's general habit of thought; but once that gesture has been made, what freedom is yours, freedom to work and to love!
T. de Chardin, LETTERS FROM A TRAVELLER (Harper & Row), p. 160.

How, practically, does one "renounce" himself?
"All that is really worthwhile is action." Why?

The Impossible Dream

Words by: Joe Darion
Music by: Mitch Leigh

To dream the impossible dream
To fight the unbeatable foe
To bear with unbearable sorrow
To run where the brave dare not go
To right the unrightable right
To love pure and chaste from afar
To try when your arms are too weary
To reach the unreachable star.
This is my quest:
To follow that star
No matter how hopeless
No matter how far
To fight for the right
Without question of foes;
To be willing to march into hell
For a heavenly goal;
And I know

I think I love you!

If I'd only be true
To this glorious quest
That my heart
Will lie peaceful and calm
When I'm laid to my rest
And the world will be better for this
That one man scorned and covered with scars
Still strives with his last ounce of courage
To reach the unreachable star.

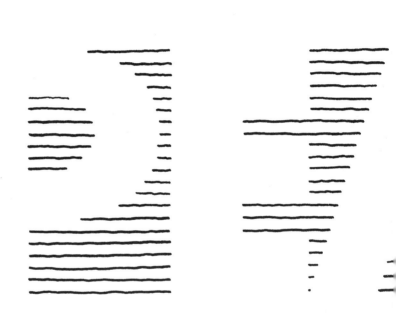

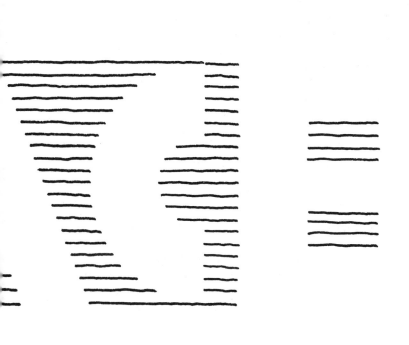

For one thing, war is outmoded.

Both economically and politically.

Certainly war once had its place. But that was
a long time ago. A very long time ago.

It does nothing now. Except anger. And kill.
And brutalize.

Forget about morality.

Although one must admit hate and violence do
tend to be moral issues.

But forget about morality.

Intelligence says it's useless. Or at least intelligence *should* say it's useless.

And the emotions say it's unnatural. Or at least
the emotions *should* say it's unnatural.

You know it's really very funny. I mean if people
believe that human life is so valuable, and that just one person
is worth more than all the objects and all the land in the world
. . . well, it's just really very funny. That's all.

There is something else that should be said about
war. It's wrong. That's where the morality comes in.

I was always taught that wrong should be avoided.
Granted, that's not quite so easy. But who ever said it was?

Who ever said it was?

PACIFISM AND THE CHRISTIAN VOCATION

**He stood before the assembly of college
students, the priest-pacifist, with the polished manner of one
used to the platform, as he deftly fielded the questions of his
audience. And I listened, bemused at the reflection of how one-
sided such encounters usually are in their total context.**

**He spoke about the goodness of man, about a
world already redeemed, about the community of saints. He
spoke about love and the strength of non-violence; about the way
men change and can change for the better. He spoke about
the Sermon on the Mount, and said that its precepts were not
for some but for all. He spoke about the true Christian role of
peacemaker. "Happy the peacemakers: they shall be called
sons of God" (Mt. v, 9).**

**And one student rose to ask what was really the
obvious question—obvious to one who waited in vain to hear
of flesh and blood in this discussion of man—and he asked:**

"But what about original sin? What about the sinfulness of man?" And the priest opened his eyes in a look of wondering innocence, and he said: "But you see, I don't believe very much in original sin." And he smiled, and all the audience smiled with him. And the student, flustered and confused, sat down. And I thought, here it is, here in this little vignette, here is the irrelevance, the unrealism of doctrinaire pacifism—that pacifism that has most been heard so much in our day and in our country, that pacifism made more popular by an unpopular war, a confusing war, but a war in which we are involved. The voice is not new, but the times are new. And the times have given it a timbre and a strength that it did not possess before. But the times could not give it the validity that it did not possess before. And this is the tragedy of doctrinaire pacifism, so appealing in the nobility of its dream to the innocence of youthful idealism, and too often proposed to them by those whose position and age does not afford the luxury of this kind of innocence.

There are many kinds of individuals, many kinds of mentalities involved in the peace-movement of our time. There are those who feel America should not be involved at all abroad, and therefore should not be involved in Vietnam either. There are those who would fight Nazism, but not communism (and some who would even welcome communism). There are those who would fight communism, but not there, not in that way (as though they had the choice of where and in what way). There are those who would not oppose the concept of war, but say that the engines of war are too fearsome today to risk any kind of conflict. There are those who, in pitying the individuals, forget the masses, or in pitying the masses, forget the world and the future. There are these and more, but these are not my concern at present. My concern at present is the pacifist, the one who rejects violence, the one who speaks of non-violence as the universal and univocal Christian obligation— the Catholic pacifist. "But, you see, I don't believe very much in original sin."

Leave the theology out of it. Look merely at man as he is. Look at the human condition. Who was it who said, long ago, that if the doctrine of original sin had not been revealed, it would have to be invented? President Johnson said that every cannon, every tank, every battleship bears mute witness to man's failure to be reasonable. I would add that every policeman, every prison, yet, and even every confessional points an accusing finger at the sinfulness of man.

"I don't believe very much in original sin."

A colonel once said that any reasonable man who had witnessed the havoc of war, the horror of war, could not but be pacific. But that reasonable men, confronting the reality of the world, could not be pacifists.

From the time of the Sermon on the Mount, and even before, there has been a constant tradition of non-violence within our tradition. Just as there has been a constant tradition of evangelical poverty and of virginity and of obedience. These have always been recognized as special vocations within and for the Christian community—as personal vocations. As has happened with each of these other injunctions of the Christian ideal, doctrinaire pacifism is but one more of the repetitious aberrations that would isolate one or the other of these elements into a new idol of unreality.

It seems ironic that an age that has seen Christianity re-formulate and re-emphasize its commitment to the world, should also foster a movement that would relegate Christianity to the shadow area of a dream world. Christ had said: "Go, sell all that you have and give to the poor, and come, follow Me." And men through the ages have responded literally to this appeal, but not in a doctrinaire way that would deny the truth and value even of wealth and the things that wealth can achieve. For it is a fact that our civilization, with its strengths and its weaknesses, could not be imagined without wealth and the things that wealth makes possible.

Christ had said: "If a man takes you to law and would have your tunic, let him have your cloak as well." And through the ages there have been men who have responded literally to this call, who have listened to St. Paul: "How dare one of your members take up a complaint against another in the lawcourts of the unjust instead of before the saints?" (I Cor. vi, 1). Yet our civilization, with all its strengths and weaknesses, could not exist were it not for the law and the courts of law and the possibilities that these alone give that sinful men might live in reasonable harmony.

Christ had said: "Do not worry about tomorrow: tomorrow will take care of itself. Each day has enough troubles of its own" (Mt. vi, 34). And through the ages men have responded literally to this call. Yet our world could not have come into being with all its achievements, with its growing and active share in the creativity of God, without long-range planning, investments, savings, insurance, and the full complement of the instrumentalities of human providence.

And Christ had said: "If anyone hits you on the right cheek, offer him the other as well" (Mt. v, 39). And through the ages men have responded literally to this call. Yet our world could not have come into being were it not for force and the strength of force and even at times violence or the threat of violence.

When soldiers, those agents of war and guarantors of peace, came to John the Baptist, they were not told to put aside their arms. They were told to bear them justly: "No intimidation! No extortion! Be content with your pay!" (Lk. iii, 14).

One of the first Gentiles to be admitted to the Christian community in the Apostolic Age, under the immediate direction of the Spirit, was a centurion—a soldier—whose name was Cornelius. "One of the centurions of the Italica cohort stationed in Caesarea was called Cornelius. He and the whole of his household were devout and God-fearing, and he gave generously to Jewish causes and prayed constantly to God . . . His offering of prayers and alms . . . has been accepted by God" (Acts x, 1).

In the persecution of Galerius and Diocletian, it was soldiers, Christians of the Imperial Army, who were the first targets, according to Eusebius.

And so, by the time Augustine developed his currently unpopular doctrine of a just war, this was not the beginning of a new tradition in Christianity. It was not the rationalization of a late aberration that was to burden the Christian community for 1,500 years. It was a serious effort to face the reality of the world from the vantage point of the Christian ideal, to express the tension that the Christian must always embrace in confronting the world, as he seeks to make his Christianity relevant by coming to grips with what is, in order to make it better. St. Thomas develops the Augustinian ideal as follows: ". . . among true worshippers of God, those wars are not sinful which are waged with the earnest desire for peace . . . The precepts of the Sermon on the Mount are always to be preserved for the purpose of forming a state of mind, in terms of which a man is always prepared not to resist or defend himself if there be not need. But there are times when other actions are demanded for the common good, even the good of those against whom he fights . . . Those who wage a just war intend peace. This is why Augustine says, 'Peace is not sought that one might engage in war; war is waged that peace might be achieved. Be, then, peaceful in fighting that you might bring those against whom you fight to peace!' " (S.T., II–II 40).

And so it has been through the centuries as sinful age after sinful age groped its way, through the Christ-light, and in the real world, in search of its own redemption, always hopeful, always failing, always growing, seeking constantly for Christ, always facing resolutely the reality that is sinful man.

Each new age has brought new horror to the art of war. Each new age took step after painful step towards the elimination of war. Now, for perhaps the first time in the history of the world, a century that has witnessed the two greatest tragedies of war has also seen men eschew war as an instrument of national policy. But it has also seen men who have given but lip service to this ideal, and this is their sin. A new step has been taken, but we are far from the final one. "Insofar as men are sinful, the threat of war hangs over them, and hang over them it will until the return of Christ" (Vat. II). Men have embraced the ideal of a world community under the rule of law. But still sin plagues their every step—their own sin, as well as that of others. And so they continue to grope, to fail, unmindful of the exhortation: "To the extent that men vanquish sin by a union of love, they will vanquish violence as well, and make these words come true: 'They shall beat their swords into plowshares and their spears into pruning hooks.' " And because they have refused to love, the pope of peace, whose emblem was the dove, still working for peace, uttered these words, the echoes of the centuries: "Every war of aggression against those goods which the Divine Plan for peace obliges men unconditionally to respect and guarantee, and accordingly to protect and defend, is a sin, a crime, an outrage against the Majesty of God, the Creator and Ordainer of the world.

"A people threatened with an unjust aggression, or already its victim, may not remain passively indifferent if it would think and act as befits Christians. Still more does the solidarity of the family of nations forbid others to behave as mere spectators in an attitude of apathetic neutrality. Who will ever measure the harm already caused in the past by such indifference to war of aggression, which is quite alien to the Christian instinct? . . . It has only reassured and encouraged the authors and fomentors of aggression . . ."

John XXIII, beloved of all, spoke strongly of the irrationality of war. He said: "Mutual trust alone serves peace." But where does mutual trust exist today? Indeed, where can it exist today? Where is the community of the world, under the rule of law? The pacifist would tell us, "The burden of trust is ours. Create it. Disarm! Manifest to men that you love them, and they will love you." But his Church, even in these latter days, says: "Everyone must labor to put an end at last to the arms race, and to make a true beginning of disarmament, *not indeed a unilateral disarmament,* but one proceeding at an equal pace according to agreement, and *backed up by authentic and workable safeguards"* (emphasis added). The pacifist would say: "Withdraw! Manifest your good intentions by pulling out of Vietnam. Prove your desire for peace." His pope says: "Let *all* those responsible strive to bring about those necessary conditions which will lead men to lay down their arms at last . . . This peace must rest on justice and the liberty of mankind, and take into account the rights of individuals and communities; otherwise it will be shifting and unstable." This is the folly of dreams vs. the wisdom of reality.

Yet, apart from the bizarre appeal of the doctrinaire, the reality of the pacific vocation remains a truth of the Christian community. The individual vocation, the personal commitment to the non-violent ideals of the Sermon on the Mount can be especially meaningful today. Just as the personal commitments to a genuine evangelical poverty and to virginity are especially meaningful today. For those who embrace these special vocations are witnesses to the conscience of the Christian and of the world community, that in their quest for life and abundance and progress, there are other values as well, even of ultimately greater importance. Just as the virgin could not seriously exhort all men to accept the vocation of virginity, but rather to examine themselves and their attitudes towards their sexuality, and just as the evangelically poor man could not seriously expect all the world to follow in his footsteps without involving all the world in ruin, but rather to examine, each in his own conscience, the genuinity of their embrace of that spirit of poverty which is incumbent upon all, so also the one who would embrace non-violence should not seriously expect all the world to embrace his way, but to examine seriously whether its use of arms is indeed consonant with

135

the spirit of peace that would only wage war reluctantly, for the sake of peace.

Daniel F. X. Meenan, "Pacifism and the Christian Vocation," SACRED HEART MESSENGER, February 1967.

Meenan says "Leave the theology out of it. Look merely at man as he is. Look at the human condition." Does the pacifist deny the human condition, that people are hungry and, as a last resort, will use violence to get both land and sustenance?

Is the pacifist impractical, hoping that peace will come without fighting for it and preserving it—with armies if necessary? Or is he the most practical of all, realizing that peace has never been a by-product of war, or at least a durable by-product?

"Mutual trust alone serves peace." What are the deterrents to mutual trust that exist today?

"Let all those responsible strive to bring about those necessary conditions which will lead men to lay down their arms at last . . ." Who are those responsible?

What is the basis of non-violence?

STUDENT VIEWS FOR THE WAR

Patricia Saust, 21 of Arlington Heights, Ill., senior at the University of Illinois in Champaign. "I think we should quit fooling around in Vietnam and get down to business. The war is dragging on—some say it might go on for 20 years. I think everyone is getting sick of it. We should use progressive bombing tactics. We have the equipment to win the war and we should quit messing around. I think we lost the Korean War because we were there too long. I think we should go out for total victory—forget any peace treaty."

Steve Rigsby, 16, of Richmond, Va., junior in high school. "My father and my grandfather fought in war. I think I should fight for peace if necessary. You should face it. It's a duty you have to give to your country. I'm living right now in freedom. Why shouldn't I fight for my children's freedom? You're fighting for children to come. If you don't like communism, why let them grow up in communism?"

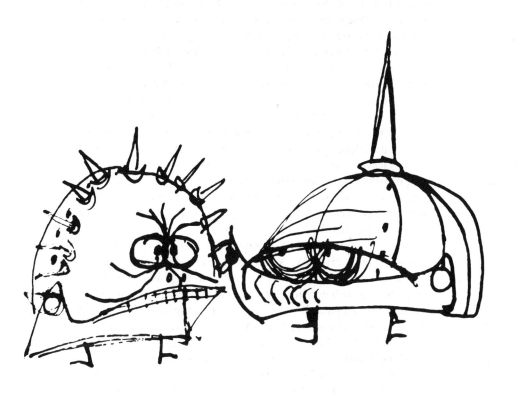

I don't know who you are, but I hate you!

Sandra Lafe, 20, of Gibsonia, Pa., senior at Chatham College, Pittsburgh, Pa. "I don't think we can defend our participation in the war in Vietnam on moral grounds. We have a pragmatic purpose—to establish the kind of government in Saigon that would be favorable to the United States. This war has riled up the domestic situation. The citizens don't seem to be behind the war in Southeast Asia as they were in World War II or the conflict in Korea. Our goals in this war, it seems to me, are hazy. Yet I favor being in the war since we already are in it. But it is not a war of ideologies but rather one in which we hope to present a picture of our foreign policy."

John K. Powless, 17, of Marion, Ill., high school senior. "We are attempting to limit the spread of communism in the underdeveloped countries of the world. We were asked by South Vietnam for help and there is no reason I can see why we should withdraw. Many South American governments are susceptible to communism. If we stay in Vietnam and achieve an honorable peace, I think it will check the spread of communism in this hemisphere."

Phelps (Mike) Riley, 20, of Gladwyne, Pa., a junior at Yale University, New Haven, Conn. "My point on Vietnam is sort of counter to student activist philosophy. I subscribe to our policies in Vietnam. We are committed to the war and it is an obligation to carry out that commitment. As a male citizen, I, like any other, am obligated to serve in the armed forces, if drafted. Many have declared that we are in the wrong and should abandon our position, but few, if any, have come forward with a meaningful plan of action to effect such a withdrawal. Until such a plan is put forward, I would not change my views. A former member of my class at Yale was killed in Vietnam Feb. 17."

Paul Penland, 17, Dallas, senior at W. T. White High School, president of the Young Republican Club at his high school. "I'm all for it. If anything, it should be escalated. Everyone worries about civilians being accidentally killed, but that's the way the cookie crumbles; that's the way war is. I think we should send more men over and we need to send more bombing raids over North Vietnam. Draft card burners and all that Mickey Mouse should be the first to go."
YOUTH QUAKE p. 20.

*What are the main arguments in favor of either
remaining in or escalating the war in Vietnam?*
How do you evaluate these arguments?

The January 1967 issue of Ramparts *magazine
contains photos of children in Vietnam who have lost limbs,
had their chins melted by napalm onto their chests, and other,
if it is possible to imagine, even more pathetic horrors. Can
morality encompass intentional perversion of the human form and
its dignity, even in the name of freedom, even in the name of
love?*
*Can the dehumanization of a man to the point
where violence is a matter of everyday affairs be a part of some
lesser evil? What, then, is the greater evil?*

You call the argument emotional. Satiric cartoons
and an admittedly melodramatic picture of a girl with her body
mutilated. We're sorry. When one is angry—and we are very
angry—one has a tendency to become emotional. Thank God
we still have emotions left. And a small sense of what is right
and what is terribly wrong.

War is a moral issue, simply because it pro-
foundly affects the morality of a man. If you are made to slaughter
cattle every day in a meat factory, your abhorrence of the
act will eventually subside into indifference, and you will quickly
become anesthetized to it all.

Now everybody knows we need meat (and that
all Communists must be killed because they're not people—
they're animals, or something else, but certainly not people. And
besides, they're going to take over the world). So the slaughter-
house routine is justified, and the man, who now does his work
diligently (and sometimes even wins medals for it), is self-
satisfied in the morality of what he is doing.

You see the analogy. Granted, Vietnam is one
meat factory where the cattle fight back, and many times more
savagely. But regardless of how you view it, this war has served
to dehumanize the American soldier and the people at home
whom he is purportedly fighting for. Violence is accepted as a
part of life, both intellectually and emotionally. And what may
have once shocked, now is received with new understanding—
that unfortunately, this is the way things are, and there is

139

nothing anyone can do about it (except, of course, drop the legendary Bomb and put an end to violence once and for all).

We even go so far as to laud violence, and fashion heroes out of those who administer it. A movie like *The Dirty Dozen* serves it up *à la carte* to the average American who has sat and watched the six o'clock news on television, replete with bleeding children, maimed women, and dead soldiers who died for real and not for a camera take. After that, fictitious terror is mere pablum.

TORMENT FOR EVERYONE

Again—our understandable but hazardous ignorance. Our ignorance stems not from a need for more facts, but from a failure to integrate and apply the facts we already have, not from a lack of knowledge but from a lack of understanding; not from unawareness of our needs but from confusion about our priorities. Our general tendency is still to approach every issue on a simple quantitative, one-plus-one-plus-one basis, to see everything in singularities. We aren't living in that kind of world. No leadership group, no matter how clever or how impeccably moral, can cope with the problems of our time on a piecemeal basis. We have to see the multi-faceted dimensions of every issue. We have to trace out the intertwining relationships which tie together so many of our problems. We have to seek for and accept the diverse sources of knowledge and understanding we must draw upon if we are to find meaningful solutions.

We have to be able to say that no one man or nation can solve our problems. No one military power or coalition of military powers can solve our problems. No one ideological system can solve our problems. But, the combined, integrated intelligence of Mankind can, with our newly developed technological skills and facilities.

Those solutions must rest upon thorough, comprehensive analysis of needs and of the resources available to meet those needs. They must have general acceptability to all men regardless of their vast individual and cultural differences. They must depend upon reasonable agreement and not upon coercion. Above all, the real solutions must be based upon an in-depth understanding of the human being, the realization

140

that each man is part of a Mankind Body, that he shares both needs and hopes and evolutionary capabilities with all other human beings, and that his advancement is interwoven with the advancement of every other man.

World Institute Council, Julius Stulman, Pres.

What is this "hazardous ignorance"?
Why is an understanding of the human being so vital in reaching a solution to the war?
". . . his [man's] advancement is interwoven with the advancement of every other man." How is this basic concept the precursor of peace?

WAR CRUSHES HUMAN DEVELOPMENT

If all we have then is "deterrence" to keep them at peace, then the world hangs on a precipice the atmosphere of which is one of human alienation—one that crushes most forms of human development. At any moment, the taut wire of so-called equilibrium can be snapped by accident, escalation, miscalculation or social conditioning. (Some "game theorists" for example feel that preparation for "war" is essential for the growth of Western knowledge. It's inevitable, they feel, so why not get ready for it in the most efficient manner?) It is easy to understand this acceptance of the inevitability of nuclear disaster if we stop to estimate the extent of the warfare culture that so much of the world tolerates or is paralyzed into accepting. Modern society can condition people for almost anything. President Kennedy had to remind us that "the world's atomic stockpile contains the equivalent of 10 tons of TNT for every human being on the globe." We call this "overkill." Perhaps an even stronger jolt to our dulled sensitivities is the relaxed breathing that accompanies discussion on "tactical nuclear warheads"—to defoliate the jungle as we are told. The average force of such weapons is 100,000 tons of TNT—or 5 times the power of the bomb that destroyed Hiroshima in the second World War.

But the tragedy is compounded, for even as we hustle with a shredded conscience through an increasingly urbanized world—about 70 percent of the U.S. is urbanized, a real index card world where skyscrapers look like metal file

141

cabinets—human desires and development are stunted by the real possibility of world annihilation, to say nothing of its financial delinquency. The blasphemy of this was sharply drawn by war correspondent Robert Sherrod in a recent issue of Life magazine when he said:

"It's costing the U.S. $400,000 to kill a Viet-Cong soldier . . . In World War II our fighter planes cost approximately $40,000. Today's F-4 Phantom jets go for $2.5 million."

Sixty-five percent of our annual budget (i.e. about $70 billion) is slotted for military expenditures. By contrast, last year's poverty budget was $1.5 billion and foreign aid's was approximately $2.8 billion. Domestically we have a "depleted society"—fewer and fewer MD's, loss of some industries to foreign competition, e.g. Underwood (Olivetti), Studebaker (Mercedes-Benz). Our welfare programs—how outdated that concept is!—rank behind those of several other countries. Our waters and air remain polluted; most of our cities have become faceless in the wake of military and industrial demands on research. Black people continue to suffer more (e.g. they are drafted more quickly and abundantly).

"War Crushes Human Development," DIALOGUE, May–June 1967.

"Modern society can condition people for almost anything." Like what for instance?

What does the word "defoliate" mean in reality? What are its consequences? It's all too easy to hide behind four syllable words, when what you really mean to say is scorch the land and burn the trees till there is only charred stumps and ash.

What are some things which could be done with the money being used for "military expenditures"?

"A report from Washington has it that the United States government has spent 850 billion dollars for war during a period of twenty years.

Translated into what good these dollars could have done for the improving of man instead of his destruction:

For those twenty years the medical and dental care of all the people could have been underwritten.

In addition 100 billion dollars would have been

How can honorable men
cope with a ruthless enemy?

He is fanatical, diabolic, inhuman.

Stern measures are necessary. Fight fire with fire!

We must learn to
think as he thinks.

Plot and scheme
as he does.

Act as he acts. Hate as he hates.

available to clear up the nation's slum areas, and 60 billion dollars to clear the nation's rivers and lakes from pollution.

This would have left 150 billion dollars which would have covered the total cost of operating for all the colleges in this nation during the twenty-year period."
"The Cost of War," CHANGE 3, 1966.

THE HABIT OF LYING

"In the actual world we are living in," says Marcel, "it is impossible not to recognize that making war is linked to lying . . . lying to others and lying to oneself . . .

"A person who is not lying to himself can hardly fail to observe that in its modern forms war is a disaster from which no counter balancing advantage can be reaped . . .

"It is only through organized lying that we can hope to make war acceptable to those who must wage or suffer it . . . As soon as people (that is to say, the State or political party or a faction or a religious sect or whatever it may be) claim of me that I commit myself to a warlike action against other human beings whom I must, as a consequence of my commitment, be ready to destroy, it is very necessary from the point of view of those who are influencing me that I lose all awareness of the individual reality of the being whom I may be led to destroy.

"In order to transform him into a mere impersonal target, it is absolutely necessary to convert him into an abstraction: *the* Communist, *the* anti-Fascist, *the* Fascist, and so on." (It might be noted here how often we read in the dispatches from Vietnam that today "our side" killed so and so many "Communists," never men; and one can assume that the dispatches from "their side" report so and so many "imperialists" killed, never American men. Brutality is noble, so long as it is a "Communist" or an "imperialist" who is killed or crippled.)
D. McDonald, Center for Study of Democratic Institutions.

What does Marcel mean by "organized lying"?
One man has said of the war: "Because I have heard so many lies I no longer recognize the truth." Is there any real truth to be recognized about this war?

In order to protect our cherished freedoms you won't mind
a few restrictions, if you're loyal.

PEACE AND CHURCH AND COUNTRY

If churches, and we are the churches, are to
magnify the moral voice of our nation, they must teach, better
than they do now, that man must love his neighbor. Charity must
guide the judgments we make on friend and foe, on presidents
or foreign leaders, on senators or editors. The hawk has no right
to hate the Vietnamese, North or South; the dove has no
right to speak of presidents or generals with ridicule or insult.
D. Herr, OVERVIEW, Aug. 1, 1967.

*Before there is peace between nations, what must
come first?*

Don't be fooled. The "peacenik" radicals
screaming for Americans to get out of Vietnam often pose as
religious pacifists, using such names as "The Catholic Worker,"
"Catholic Peace Fellowship," etc. But these ultra-leftist traitors
have no connection whatsoever with the Catholic Church. They
are not religious groups, but are pro-Communist action
organizations hoping to seize control of the United States.
"The Talk of the Town," THE NEW YORKER, Dec. 24, 1966, p. 23.

What do statements such as this accomplish?

Decent men and women accept moral
responsibility for what they do . . . and for the things they fail
to do. All of us fail at times to do what we know is right, but
even in these failures we acknowledge our responsibility—unless
we are moral juveniles.

The American society is truly pluralistic in its
religious life. It is clear, nevertheless, that the Jewish-Christian
vision of man's personal dignity and responsibility sweeps like a
channel current through our history and social structures.

In this religious tradition we find landmark
convictions: a God who is personally concerned with the affairs
of men; the responsibility to this God of each individual man;
the conviction that, through God, the action of the individual can

146

accomplish mysterious, immeasurable effects in the history of man.

If we acknowledge these truths as real, we cannot escape the burden of resolving our conscience on a moral crisis such as now confronts us in Vietnam.

And modern man asks himself: Does religion have anything hard and real and significant to say about these evils of our day? If the testimony of religion is limited to pious platitudes—and to the commandments of personal morality— then it can hardly be taken as a serious force in these great movements of our time.

"Vietnam and Personal Conscience," AVE MARIA, May 27, 1967, pp. 6–7.

"Decent men and women accept moral responsibility for what they do . . ." If you are a soldier, you must do the work of a soldier. To what extent is a soldier, any soldier, responsible?

"I have a responsibility for my government." What is that responsibility?

"For modern man—particularly the young —peace and social justice have become the tests of religious relevance." What does this mean?

What constitutes "responsible dissent"? How is it best manifested?

"I must not abdicate my responsibility." In what ways do men do just that?

What is the absurdity in talking of "kill-ratios"? Is not the very term absurd?

What is the difficulty in establishing the facts? How do they contradict? Give examples.

"No reasonable man would deny that we owe some kind of loyalty to our nation." What constitutes loyalty?

"We can keep our principles clear." How do your basic principles measure up with your attitude toward the war? Are some things totally immoral, regardless of "worthy purposes" behind them?

Do you have a working, practical judgment regarding the general morality of our involvement in the Vietnamese war?

What is it—at least at this point?

It's our world and we're stuck with it.

Afterthoughts on a Napalm-Drop
on Jungle Villages Near Haiphong

All was still.
The sun rose through the silver pine boughs,
Over sleeping green-straw huts,
Over cool rice ponds,
Through the emerald jungles,
Into the sky.

The men rose and went out into the fields and ponds,
The women set the pots on the fire, boiling rice and jungle berries,
    and some with baskets went for fish.
The children played in the streams and danced through the weeds.

Then there was the flash—
Silver and gold,
Silver birds flying,
Golden water raining.
The rice ponds blazed with new water.
The jungles burst into gold and sent up little birds of fire.
Little animals with fur of flame.

Then the children flamed.
Running—their clothes flying like fiery kites.
Screaming—their screams dying as their faces seared.
The women's baskets burned on their heads.
The men's boats blazed on the rice waters.
Then the rains came.

A rag, fire black, fluttered.
A curl of smoke rose from a lone rice stream.
The forest lay singed, seared.
A hut crumbled.

And all was still.

        Listen, Americans,
        Listen, clear and long.
        The children are screaming
        In the jungles of Haiphong.
VENTURE, Feb. 1967.

Loaves and Fishes

And there were five loaves and two fishes,
and they were to feed them to many thousands.

They will not be enough, they will not be enough,
cried the small men who wanted to feed them.
But there were other men who saw
there would be more than enough,
and wept.

And there were five loaves and two fishes,
to feed the multitude, to feed the hunger
of unknown women and children.
Feed my sheep, the man had said,
and they fed them fire.
Feed my sheep,
and the numbers they fed were in the thousands.

And there were five loaves and two fishes,
and the loaves they were stainless,
and the fish were of steel,
and all of them were without a spot.

And there were five loaves and two fishes,
and they were fed to the thousands,
who were scattered into fragments,
who wept, who bled.
And the fragments gathered into boxes and baskets
were without number
and filled the ground of that place.

And those who had fed them saw the thing,
that it was good,
and they went back the way they had come,
into their own country.
Michael Dennis Browne, LISTENING, Spring 1967, pp. 128–129.

LORD, HAVE MERCY

It was our idea that I should write about the theological implications of hunger, but I found that I could not do it. What follows are the preparatory notes which I have collected over the last weeks.

1. Today 15,000 people died of hunger.
2. Today probably 10,000 children died of hunger.
3. I said to my wife at breakfast, "Why do you eat that old piece of bread? We don't have a famine here." She smiled.
4. My son of three: "I don't want to eat. I don't want to eat again." My wife: "You are not hungry because you have eaten too much candy."
5. Today probably 10,000 children died of hunger.
6. The friends of Job said to him, "In famine He will redeem you from death." Who wants to be a friend of Job?
7. The Church has prayed for centuries, "Give us today our daily bread." When that prayer became problematic because bread was also secured without prayer, the theologians said that a better translation was, "Give us today our bread for tomorrow." And then the planners took away the need for *that* prayer. If there is no bread tomorrow, we'll eat something else!
8. To pray "Give us our daily bread" and to forget to share it when our prayer is answered, is blasphemy. For the rich and overfed: Don't call down judgment on yourselves. Let's abolish the Lord's Prayer.
9. Bonhoeffer said, "Only he who shouts for the Jews may sing Gregorian chants." Implication: only he who shares his bread may come to the Lord's table. Let's abolish the Eucharist.
10. Probably 10,000 children died today of hunger.
11. The principle of the welfare state, in which all citizens share the food, is now accepted by all. Few people would like to abolish *that* national planning. Most people are willing to pay taxes for *that* reason. We take responsibility for the hungry in our land!
12. To establish a welfare system for the whole world, in which all have sufficient to eat, is nonsense, political suicide, optimism. Nobody would like to have that planned *internationally*. Nobody would be so crazy as to pay taxes for *that*. We don't take responsibility for the hungry of the world!
13. Lord, we thank Thee that we are born in a land of plenty,

where we can destroy some of the surplus food we do not need. We thank Thee, O Lord, that we are not hungry, that our children do not rot away in famine but have more than they can possibly eat. Lord, we are grateful for democracy, that we are given a share in the decision-making process and so receive new responsibilities. We thank Thee that we have the knowledge and the means to feed all. O Lord, feed Thou the hungry. Amen.

14. From a leaflet: "An absolute priority for our church is to build new sanctuaries in new neighborhoods. Let us express the depth of our faith in the beauty of God's house."

15. See 2.

16. Plato wanted to have begging condemned by law.

17. Cum esuriente panem suum dividat (Stoa).

18. The Gnostics taught that hunger was a blessing because it liberated people from their desires and brought them closer to God. A pseudo-Gnostic argument: Do we know what we do when we give aid to hungry countries?

19. During the winter of 1944–1945 I was hungry. We lived on a bowl of soup and one piece of bread a day. One day my mother had some pies and made me take one to my grandmother. I ate it all on the way, and told my parents that I had been attacked on the road. I loved my grandmother, but hunger is stronger than love.

20. Jeremiah is a hunger prophet. The word he uses means famine. It is one of three eschatological punishments God sends to the unfaithful.

21. The couple arrested in Amsterdam in 1945 for having eaten part of their own child, who had died of hunger, were acquitted without trial. After they had been fed by the police, they showed immense remorse.

22. Hunger in the Old Testament is differently understood, according to the situation of the hungry. It can be divine punishment; it can be a redemptive humiliation; it can also be the promising situation God will visit when He comes. In other words, the Old Testament did not know what to do about it either. In any case, it was terrible.

23. The bell rang during that winter we had nothing to eat. On the doorstep stood one of the most respected men in our town, a Professor of Law. He had resigned because of the anti-Jewish law in education. Looking at me through his gold-rimmed glasses, he very kindly—and very remotely at the same time—

inquired, "Would you ask your mother whether she has any potato peelings left? I am very hungry." The humiliation of being rich.

24. In the Old Testament, hunger may contain a promise but it is never a blessing (Strack-Billerbeck).

25. The striking thing about the first temptation in the desert is not that Jesus immediately knew a Bible text to resist the Tempter, but that He remembered it although He was hungry.

26. "For the first time in human history," said J. F. Kennedy, "we have the means to feed all: we lack only the willingness to share."

27. See 2.

28. The greatest problem to be overcome in relation to hunger is nationalism. Not in its original meaning as "shared responsibility and shared power for the whole nation," but in its present perverted forms, which are either messianic, aggressive or defensive. A messianic, aggressive or defensive nationalist is a murderer.

29. When Jesus said, "Blessed are the hungry," what exactly did He mean? Kittel's dictionary on the New Testament says, "The hungry are the people who lack what they need innerly and outwardly to live a life as God wanted it, and who turn to Him because they cannot help themselves. Only those hungry people find God's help. They are not a social or religious group which already existed. The Beatitudes, like the promise of the Psalms, are ultimately words of Salvation, which create the hungry." Am I dumb, or does the dictionary here say that when God sees a starving human being He first wants to know whether he also inwardly longs for God's word? See 2. I don't understand the Beatitudes very well and they probably allow for more than one exegesis. *I* think that Jesus was referring to a sort of FAO, which His followers would make work. He may also have been powerless and unable to give anything else but a blessing.

30. One thing is clear. The damnation of the rich is as lucid as the promise to the hungry.

31. Why did we never put John 6 (the feeding of the five thousands) into our Eucharistic texts? The relation between the Lord's table and the world's hunger is considerably more meaningful than the whole intercommunion debate.

32. J. C. Hoekendijk in *Youth* 6. "Intercommunion is about nations, not denominations."

153

33. It is interesting—for want of a better word—that the *rich* nations always say, "The poor countries should do something about their own structures, about their birthrate, about their infrastructure." When there is a famine somewhere, the rich are amazed that the distribution of their food programs is done so sloppily.

34. Reflecting on the experience of the absence of God. Why should we be allowed to experience His presence rather than the damnation of the rich?

35. "God is dead. He died in our time, in our existence," yes, today, with 14,999 others. See Pascal, *Penseés* 372 (533).

36. What should the prodigal son do, when he is starving to death and he knows that his father has given the authority over his house and his food to his servants?

37. A parable: There was once a man who had a rich property. He gave it to his children to care for. Because the father loved his children, he left on a long journey and gave them real freedom to organize his property their own way. Now part of that property was cultivated and another part was not. The sons who lived on the richer part built fences to defend their section from the others who lived on the wild parts. They led a good life themselves, and once in a while threw some food over the fence so that the other children at least knew how good life could be. Then the children on the other side of the fence sent a delegation to their brothers and said, "Teach us how to cultivate our soil, and while we learn, share your riches with us so that we do not die." But their brothers said, "Go away: there is not enough for all of us. Learn to till the soil your- selves." The others said, "We will do that, but we have no tools to till the soil. Help us with your tools." But their brothers responded, "We cannot do that because we need all we have if we want to keep up our standard of living. We'll give you a few tools, and with them you can make your own." The others said, "In order to make tools we need money. Buy what we have reaped on our land and we shall buy our own tools from you." Their brothers replied, "But we don't need prod- ucts. If you sell them to us our economy will be disrupted." The others said, "But then what shall we do; our wives and our children are dying." Their brothers said, "It will take time." The others, seeing that their brothers did not really want to help them, stormed the fence, broke it down, took the food they needed and killed all the brothers who resisted them. Then the

owner of the property returned, and was both angry and sad. To the surprise of the children who had lived behind their fences, he put the others in charge of the whole property and forgave them their violence. Will the sons of men remember what had been done to them?

38. One of the hardest hermeneutical problems comes from the fact that the Bible is pre-democratic. It speaks in terms of charity because the power to attack a problem at its political roots was still in the hands of the kings and rulers. What we need badly today is a political exegesis of *agape*.

39. A theological treatment of hunger is a political treatment of hunger.

40. If the rich keep considering their wealth as a right, the poor will consider their vengeance as justice.

41. In the language of the poor, hunger is injustice, not fate; in the language of the rich, hunger is greed, not tragedy.

42. In the ten commandments, in the prophets and in parts of the New Testament, more emphasis is given to the No, to injustice than to the motives for justice. The reason for that amazingly negative approach is in the covenant relationship between God and His people. God's faithfulness is the basis on which this imbalance is bearable.

43. Searching for theological evaluations of hunger means that the rich must ponder conversion and *Büsse* (Luther), penitence. For the poor, it means pondering what hope means biblically. For both, love and faith form the context of their thinking.

44. Kraemer has distinguished between *ardor theologicus* and *rabies theologica.* Kraemer would have judged the difference in terms of "biblical realism."

45. The concept of the Church of the Poor may, in the long run, be the most important thing the Vatican Council produced— and left unused. Archbishop Camara wrote about it under the title *What the Council Could Not Say* (IDOC, D.66-2).

46. The important things about hunger today are said by the international organizations like UNCTAD and FAO. The Church does not have to help these organizations to find a Theology of Development, but with an army of trained politicians who, in the words of Jeremiah, "work for the *shalom* of the city and pray to the Lord for it" (Jer. 29).

47. Kyrie eleison . . .

A. Van Den Heuvel, "Kyrie Eleison," THE DEVELOPMENT APOCALYPSE, edited by S. C. Rose (Youth Department World Council of Churches), pp. 145–150.